D0232510

WITHDRAWN

BOSTON UNIVERSITY
African Research Studies
Number 4

Studies in

EAST AFRICAN
HISTORY

NORMAN R. BENNETT
Boston University

BOSTON UNIVERSITY PRESS
Boston, Massachusetts
1963

Studies in East African History

To
SIR JOHN GRAY
For His Many Kindnesses
During Our Stay in
Zanzibar

Preface

The four studies in this collection are the result of visits to African, European and American libraries and archives from 1958 to 1960. They do not revolve around any one theme, but rather seek to recount various aspects of the history of East Africa that have not been told in detail before. Mirambo, one of the most important African leaders of Tanganyika in the nineteenth century, has never had a serious biography. The Holy Ghost Mission in Tanganyika and the American influence in Zanzibar from 1865 to 1915 suffer from a similar lack. Finally, the study on Mwinyi Mtwana is meant to draw attention to the myriad relationships between the Sultan of Zanzibar and those in Africa who considered themselves under his suzerainty — a subject still largely untouched by students of East African history.

The author is indebted for aid in research and writing to: Mr. Marion Brewington of the Peabody Museum; Mr. Paul Blanchette, formerly of the Essex Institute and now of the Peabody Museum; Mrs. Charles Potter of the Essex Institute; Dr. Marcel Luwel of the Musée de l'Afrique Centrale, Tervuren; Professor J. Stengers of the Université Libré, Bruxelles; Miss Rosemary Keen of the Church Missionary Society Archives; Miss Irene Fletcher of the London Missionary Society Archives; Mr. C. Thompson of the Zanzibar Archives; Father John Hensbergen and his colleagues of the Holy Ghost Mission, Bagamoyo; Professor Daniel McCall, Professor Jeffrey Butler, and Mr. Douglas Wheeler of the African Studies Program; Dr. Philip Gulliver of the University of London; the Provincial Commissioner, Western Province, Tanganyika; Sir John Gray; Miss Marcia Wright; Mrs. Harold Marcus; Mrs. Ruth Bennett.

The greater part of the research for these studies was undertaken while the author held a Ford Foundation Fellowship; that in the Salem archives was aided by a grant from the African Studies Program. Particular thanks go to Dr. William O. Brown for generous support during their writing.

The article on Americans in Zanzibar has appeared in the Essex Institute *Historical Collections* and has been revised somewhat for its publication here.

Norman R. Bennett

Boston, Mass.
October, 1962

TABLE OF CONTENTS

  (The places marked with a question mark were deduced from
the map in Jerome Becker, *La Vie en Afrique* [Bruxelles, 1887].
The map was prepared by John Sommer.)

Mirambo of the Nyamwezi

In the last third of the nineteenth century an African leader controlled wide areas of present-day Tanganyika. His main base was at Urambo, near Tabora, and his influence reached in the west almost to Lake Tanganyika, in the north almost to Lake Victoria, and in the south to the latitude of Lake Rukwa. Thus it encompassed some of the most important central African trade routes and, consequently, the chief was courted by representatives of the various European organizations then interested in East Africa. He was Mirambo of the Nyamwezi, the "African Bonaparte,"[1] who first came to the knowledge of the outside world when H. M. Stanley, while on his expedition after Livingstone, joined the Arabs of Tabora in attacking him. Only one serious study of this important African leader has been attempted — that of Ronald J. Harvey, "Mirambo," *Tanganyika Notes and Records*, 28 (1950), 10–28. But Harvey overlooked much of the material about Mirambo's career.

I

Little is known of Mirambo's early life. Travellers of the 1870's and 1880's estimate his birth date as between 1830 and 1840. There is almost unanimity, though details vary, in the belief that Mirambo was born in the small chiefdom of Uyowa in the Nyamwezi area, an issue of the ruling family.[2] Some claim that he was the son of a slave, but this does not necessarily invalidate his claim to royalty since tradition represents Mirambo's father as adopted by the chief of Uyowa after he married his

[1] Henry M. Stanley, *How I Found Livingstone* (London, 1872), 296.
[2] Philippe Broyon-Mirambo, "Note sur l'Ouniamouezi," *Bulletin de la Société de Géographie de Marseille*, I (1877), 258; Adolphe Burdo, *Les Belges dans l'Afrique Centrale de Zanzibar au Tanganika* (Bruxelles, 1886), 22; H. Brode, *Tippoo Tib* (London, 1907), 134; E. Southon, "History." The text of Southon's "History is given in an appendix.

daughter.³   Another story was given by Stanley; he claimed Mirambo
was a usurper who seized the throne when the ruler of Uyowa died.
Stanley, however, gleaned this information from the hostile Arabs of
Tabora and it may be discounted.⁴

Writers who claim Mirambo was of lowly birth point to the fact that
he was a porter in Arab caravans to the coast as proof. It is also stated
that he was sold to an Arab in his youth,⁵ but there is no evidence of it.
In any case, to work in a caravan was a custom of long standing among
the Nyamwezi, and sons of important chiefs often took such service;
Fundikira, a ruler of the Nyamwezi of Tabora, did so before he came to
power.⁶ Mirambo made no secret of his work as a porter; he once told
a visitor that several of his trips to the coast were undertaken in caravans
that included his father.⁷ Service with the Arabs entailed no stigma,
especially in view of the claim of the famous Tippu Tip that both his
and Mirambo's grandfathers were very closely associated.⁸ Fortunately,
information on Mirambo becomes more plentiful from 1871 onwards when
more and more Europeans came into the area under his influence.⁹

About 1871, Mirambo became involved in war with the Arabs of
Tabora, a state of affairs for which various explanations are given.
Mirambo's is that after he inherited his chiefdom, the Arabs sought a
pretext to break his power. When, in about 1871, some slaves of a
wealthy Tabora Arab deserted to territory which Mirambo had recently
brought under his control, their owner sent an order to the latter to return
them at once. Mirambo took steps to do so. He was delayed, he stated,
through no fault of his own, and the Arab, accusing him of bad faith,
attacked.¹⁰

    ³ F. G. Carnochan, and H C. Adamson, *Out of Africa* (London, 1937), 114, 219;
W. C. Willoughby, "Mirambo, King of the Wanyamwezi," *The Chronicle of the London Missionary Society* (1884), 17; Jerome Becker, *La Vie en Afrique* (Bruxelles,
1887), II, 173.
    ⁴ Stanley, *Livingstone*, 268; Stanley later reversed some of his opinions — see
Henry M. Stanley, *Through the Dark Continent* (New York, 1878), I, 493.
    ⁵ Carnochan and Adamson, *Out of Africa*, 118, 220.
    ⁶ Richard F. Burton, *The Lake Regions of Central Africa* (London, 1860), I, 300.
For similar evidence relating to another famous Nyamwezi leader, see Auguste Ver-
becken, *Msiri, Roi du Carenganze* (Bruxelles, 1956), 44.
    ⁷ Broyon-Mirambo, "Note sur l'Ouniamouezi," 260.
    ⁸ Brode, *Tippoo Tib*, 134.
    ⁹ In the 1860's Tippu Tip had this to say of Mirambo: "And at this time no one
knew about Mirambo." See *Maisha ya Hamed bin Muhammed el Murjebi yaani
Tippu Tip* (Supplement to the East African Swahili Committee Journals, No. 28/2,
July 1958 and No. 29/1, Jan. 1959), 41.
    ¹⁰ Southon, "History."

Other accounts, drawn from unfriendly sources, put the blame on Mirambo. One is that Mirambo was mistreated while working in an Arab caravan; he reacted by killing the offending Arab, and his long war against the Arabs was launched.[11] In another version, the occasion for war was the failure of an Arab to pay debts owed to Mirambo. Mirambo seized one of his caravans for compensation, and hostilities began in retaliation.[12] But these reports, even if true, do not give the real causes for the long war between Mirambo and the Arabs. Friction was inevitable as Mirambo grew in power and strove to increase his share of the profits from the trade flowing through his area. And the Arabs, of course, resisted any change that would interfere with their control of commerce; an earlier African leader of Tabora, Mnywa Sere, had been broken by them for just that reason.[13]

Stanley, who was in touch with both the Arabs and Mirambo, may perhaps have come upon the event that actually started hostilities between these rivals for the trade of central Tanganyika. The Arabs' version is that Mirambo asked for their support against the Nyamwezi ruler of Tabora, Mkasiwa, a man under their influence. When the Arabs refused, Mirambo closed the trade route to Ujiji on Lake Tanganyika; negotiations failed and thus war began. On the other hand, according to Mirambo, the Arabs and Mkasiwa tried to extend their influence over him and thus forced him to fight.[14] It seems, therefore, that Mirambo wished to be regarded as the paramount African leader in the Tabora area, but the Arabs preferred Mkasiwa. In such a situation almost any event could have triggered hostilities between Mirambo and the Arabs.

It is interesting in view of his future policy towards Mirambo that John Kirk, British representative in Zanzibar, placed the blame for this quarrel fully on the Tabora Arabs, whom he called "a set of avaricious unprincipled men, whose acts of extortion both on natives and the poorer Arabs have for some time back been complained of to Seyed Burgash." He pointed out that the Sultan had no power to compel them to act otherwise.[15] Here we have a hint of Kirk's later policy of supporting Mirambo as a means of bringing order in an area vital to the trade of Zanzibar.

[11] Adolphe Burdo, *Les Arabes dans l'Afrique Centrale* (Paris, 1885), 40.
[12] Verney Lovett Cameron, *Across Africa* (London, 1877), I, 150–51.
[13] See John Hanning Speke, *Journal of the Discovery of the Source of the Nile* (London, 1863), 9 ff.
[14] Stanley, *Dark Continent*, I, 493; Stanley, *Livingstone*, 268; Stanley's letter of 21. ix. 71 in *The New York Herald* of 9. viii. 72.
[15] Kirk to F.O., 22. ix. 71. F.O. 84/1344, Public Record Office, London.

The war itself began in August 1871. Stanley, who had just arrived
in Tabora, gives Mirambo's having stopped an Arab caravan as the actual
casus belli.[16] The Arabs, in planning their campaign, spoke of defeating
Mirambo in fifteen days, and Stanley, who had fallen under the spell of
their martial confidence, agreed to join them in their campaign. His justification was that he would thereby remove a hindrance in his search for
Livingstone.[17] A party of 2255 men, 1500 of them equipped with muskets, set off at once after Mirambo. To oppose them, Mirambo had an
estimated 1000 muskets in his own forces, and the aid of 1000 Ngoni
allies.[18]

The sequel, in which Stanley took no part, since he went down with
fever, is well-known. The Arabs won a few easy victories. Mirambo,
however, managed to ambush them when they were laden with booty,
and they beat an immediate retreat to Tabora. The Nyamwezi chief
pursued the Arabs and Stanley, killed five of the leading Arabs, burned
about one-quarter of the town, and retired. Stanley had fortified his
residence to meet attack, but it never came. With the Arabs' defeat and
despite their objections, Stanley withdrew from the struggle, for he saw
no hope of victory for their badly-led forces and, soon after, left for
Ujiji by a devious route.[19]

The war continued after Stanley's departure with Mirambo soon forced
to the defensive. He suffered a series of defeats at the hands of the Arabs
in September and the months following and when Stanley again passed
through Tabora on his return to Zanzibar, he predicted: "In a month he
will be dead of hunger."[20] Livingstone, who remained for a while in
Tabora, saw Mirambo's peril, but then reported a turn in the tide of
battle. Before this reversal Mirambo had sought terms of peace from
the Arabs, who refused and thereupon began to lose ground, their dis-
unity in waging war being the main cause of their change of fortune.
The Tabora Arabs, after all, were a community of traders and lacked the

[16] Stanley's letter of 20. ix. 71 in *The New York Herald* of 15. vii. 72.

[17] *Ibid.* After the subsequent defeat, Stanley put it this way: "I was tempted in
an unlucky moment to promise them my aid."

[18] Stanley's letter of 21. ix. 71 in *The New York Herald* of 9. viii. 72; Stanley,
Livingstone, 278–79.

[19] *Ibid.*, 281 ff; Southon, "History." An Arab there at that time reported that
Mirambo sent a special message to Stanley "to say that he would drive Bwana Stanley
back to the coast . . ." See Alfred G. Robinson to L.M.S., 13. x. 1956, Stanley-
Livingstone Tembe, Tabora.

[20] Stanley, *Livingstone*, 304, 596, 611.

organization needed for a sustained military effort. In Livingstone's words: "The success of the war is a minor consideration with all." [21]

As a consequence, a long stalemate followed, and the customary trade to the coast suffered considerably. Interruption of the normal trade channels to Zanzibar forced the Sultan of Zanzibar to action. The Arabs of Tabora called for aid in February, 1872, asserting that they were "blockaded, unable to trade and short of provisions." This demonstrated, however, one of the serious problems the Sultan's government had to meet, namely, that the pleas from Tabora for military and financial aid were belied by the fact that traders in Zanzibar, following information from their agents in Tabora, were going ahead with the outfitting of new caravans for the interior. Naturally, then, the Sultan had just cause to doubt the alleged plight of Tabora.[22]

But as hostilities continued, trade did, in fact, stop.[23] It was later claimed that from 1872 to 1875 the Arab-Mirambo war caused the price of ivory in Zanzibar to double.[24] Mirambo's fortunes in war waxed and waned: by 1873, the explorer, Cameron, who had arrived in Tabora in August, noted that only one village was left under his control and that African groups were turning to the Arabs.[25] It must be remembered, however, that these reports probably came from Arab sources. Cameron also told of a large Arab force sent from Zanzibar by the Sultan to end the war. Altogether, the Arabs in Tabora had military forces numbering up to 3000 men but rivalry between the Governor of Tabora, Said ibn Salim, two leading Arabs of the interior, Abdullah ibn Nasib and Shaykh ibn Nasib, and the commander sent by the Sultan, Amir ibn Sultan, over who should take command, prevented effective use of it.[26]

This demonstrated the fundamental weakness of the Arab power in East Africa. A group of Arabs, resident for varying periods of time in Tabora, was accustomed to keep control of their local community: they

[21] *The Last Journals of David Livingstone* (London, 1874), II, 166, 198, 208, 222.

[22] Kirk to F.O., 10. iv. 72, F.O. 84/1357, with enclosures from the Tabora Arabs.

[23] There are numerous reports on this; see for example Kirk's letter of 27. v. 73 in *Proceedings of the Royal Geographical Society*, 17 (1872–73), 337.

[24] Alison Smith, "Historical Introduction," *Maisha ya . . . Tippu Tip*, 33. For a chart of the price of ivory in Zanzibar during the nineteenth century, see Appendix II.

[25] Cameron's letters of 16. vi. 73 and 14. vii. 73, *P.R.G.S.*, 18 (1873–74), 71–3; Cameron, *Across Africa*, I, 124, 139–40, 231–32. *The New York Herald* at about this time published this odd report: "Mirambo was slain and his head stuck on a spear and borne in triumph to Tabora." No source was given. See issue of 22. iii. 73.

[26] Cameron, *Across Africa*, I, 151–54, 196; Kirk to –, 5. xii. 73, E-55, Zanzibar Archives [hereafter Z.A.].

would not bow to new leaders sent by the distant Sultan of Zanzibar, even though bringing the auxiliaries for which the Arabs had asked. Their jealousy, in the end, caused the Sultan to abandon the campaign against Mirambo. He first refused to honor any further drafts sent down from Tabora by the leading Arabs; they claimed the drafts were for legitimate expenses of defense, but he believed they were used for other purposes.[27] Then he sent an agent to investigate the actual course of events in Tabora, who returned with so unfavorable a report that he decided to withdraw his forces, absolving Amir ibn Sultan of any fault for his lack of success and praising him for doing all that was possible in a trying situation.[28] The Tabora Arabs were thus left entirely to their own devices in settling their dispute with Mirambo.

To the British agent in Zanzibar, this comedy of errors seemed to presage an end of the Sultan's claim to authority in this part of the African interior.[29]

With withdrawal of support from Zanzibar, conditions around Tabora began to improve. Mirambo now wanted peace so that he could again find an outlet for his ivory on the coast. He had also been suffering from a gunpowder blockade imposed against him on the coast by the Sultan. True, he could secure some powder through friendly tribes and from traders coming from Portuguese territory, but not enough for his needs.[30] So he despatched presents to the Sultan to mark a new era of friendship. The Sultan did not formally accept them, but he did order them sold and had the proceeds returned to Mirambo.[31] Since the usual custom in East Africa was to send presents in return, equal in value to those sent, Mirambo could interpret this as a friendly act if he desired; at the same time the wily Sultan could not be accused of bowing to the enemy.

The Arabs of Tabora then decided to act on their own to end hostilities. Mirambo was not letting Arab caravans pass in peace and the Governor of Tabora, who had long opposed the unprofitable war, sent an agent to him to conclude peace.[32] The terms are not known, but no

[27] Kirk to F.O., 17. xi. 73, F.O. 84/1376.
[28] Elton to F.O., 24. xii. 74, E–65, Z.A.; an unsigned note based on native information in E–67, *ibid.*; Smith to F.O., 31. vii. 75, E–72, *ibid.*
[29] Prideaux to F.O., 21. ix. 74, E–65, *ibid.*
[30] Kirk to F.O., 22. ix. 71, F.O. 84/1344; Prideaux to F.O., 12. i. 74, E–64, Z.A.; Cameron's letter of 4. iii. 74 in *The New York Herald* of 27. viii. 74; Euan Smith to Salisbury, 28. vi. 88, F.O. 84/1907.
[31] The unsigned note in E–67, Z.A.
[32] Southon, "History"; Smith to F.O., 31. vii. 75, E–72, Z.A.; Stanley, *Dark Continent*, I, 493.

doubt the Arabs thereafter passed through Mirambo's territory in peace on the payment of tribute in the customary East African manner.

After this, the ever-active Mirambo sought new areas to extend his influence and turned to the region between his capital, Urambo, and Lake Victoria, where Stanley met him in April 1876. It should be noted that there were Arabs travelling with Mirambo when they met.[33] As a result of the new campaign, Mirambo became a dominant chief on the route to Victoria, although frequent interventions were necessary to maintain his position.

The adroit Mirambo was able to dominate central Tanganyika because of his superior abilities in military tactics and organization. His continued victories, for one thing, were due to the mobility of his forces in war. It was his practice to lead his men quickly to the scene of action, and at dawn strike an unprepared section of the defenses. Mirambo usually led these attacks in person, thus insuring that his men conducted themselves as he required if they were to be rewarded after the battle. The troops were composed of young, unmarried men, full of enthusiasm since they knew victory would bring spoils to the valiant.

Once victorious, Mirambo usually executed the chief of the captured village. He set up a new chief, chosen always from the former ruling group so that discontent would be kept at a minimum. The new ruler had to swear allegiance to Mirambo and to promise him, as did all chiefs under his authority, a contingent of young men when he went to war. If the demands were not met, Mirambo did not hesitate to execute the recalcitrant ruler and to install a new one, but if the subject chiefs complied, they were treated favorably and were given a share in the booty from victories. A few of Mirambo's men were left in each village to insure continued loyalty.

After each battle, all the booty, in theory, was given to Mirambo, who kept about one-half of it, returning the remainder to the original holders and sharing his own surplus with those who had demonstrated conspicuous bravery and who might not have had an opportunity for plundering. Later, as the soldiers grew older, they married and settled down to enjoy the fruits of war.

Because of his many victories, Mirambo soon attracted great numbers

---

[33] *Ibid.*, 494. Cameron reported that some Arabs had offered their support to Mirambo even during the course of hostilities; Mirambo said, "Traitors once, traitors always," and had them killed. See Cameron's letter of 4. iii. 74 in *The New York Herald* of 22. viii. 74.

of vigorous men to his standard. However, they created a problem: to keep them together he had to wage continual war. European residents report that he was forced to go to war on slight pretext at times when his men were growing restless. A missionary describing Mirambo and his men as always on the move, added that they "spend their whole time in planning, preparing for, or actually engaging in a war of greater or lesser magnitude." [34] Mirambo also allied himself with warlike tribes for his campaigns, chief among them being the Ngoni of Tanganyika, although, at least in a few battles, he used contingents from the Masai. The Ngoni, however, were not dependable allies, and in his later years he was to have considerable trouble with them.[35]

Here lay Mirambo's strength and his weakness: his own military ability and an efficient fighting force of followers and allies allowed him to achieve dominance in central Tanganyika. And once he had won a victory, by a wise policy of supporting local rulers and by threat of force, he kept his territories as much under his control as could be expected in the Africa of his day. But it was an unstable balance, demanding a continuous state of war as well as a leader of Mirambo's genius, and therefore it could not outlast him.

II

In 1875, Mirambo received a European visitor when Philippe Broyon, the first European trader to go into inland Tanganyika, came to him at Urambo to see what business could be done.[36] Broyon was received in so friendly a manner that the two men soon became blood-brothers, and eventually the Swiss trader married an African woman from the chief's village. She apparently was a former slave, but Broyon, either on false information from Mirambo or in a deliberate attempt to raise his standing in Zanzibar, claimed she was Mirambo's daughter. On returning to the coast with ivory to trade for Mirambo, Broyon there spread reports of the latter's desire to meet other Europeans on peaceful terms.

[34] Southon to L.M.S., 19. ii. 80 and his "Journal" entries of 10. xi. 78 and 12. viii. 80, L.M.S. Archives, London; A. Dodgshun, "From London to Ujiji," an inserted extract from Mackay to Wigram, 13. iv. 78, *ibid.*; D. Williams, "Journal," entry of 28. iv. 80, *ibid.*; Southon, "History"; Burdo, *Tanganika*, 24; Copplestone to C.M.S., 24. vi. 79, C. A6/09, C.M.S. Archives, London; E. C. Dawson, *James Hannington* (London, 1887), 275.

[35] For the Ngoni, G. W. Hatchell, "The Angoni of Tanganyika Territory," *Tanganyika Notes and Records*, 25 (1948), 69–71.

[36] For Broyon, see the author's forthcoming article in *African Affairs*, "Philippe Broyon — Pioneer Trader in East Africa."

The next Europeans to enter Mirambo's sphere of influence were members of the large group of missionaries which invaded east central Africa in the mid-1870's. In 1876 a party from the Church Missionary Society, led by Lt. Shergold Smith, passed Urambo on its way to Lake Victoria. They did not attempt to visit Mirambo, being uncertain of the reception they would receive, but they exchanged friendly messages and laid the groundwork for future visits. Soon after, an Englishman, Joseph Morton, was dispatched inland to bring supplies to Shergold Smith. His task completed, Morton visited Mirambo on the return trip. He received the usual cordial reception and agreed to carry ivory to the coast for the Nyamwezi chief, as well as letters of friendship from him to the authorities of Zanzibar.[37]

At this time, certain events occurred at Tabora which caused the British Consul to inaugurate a new policy of closer relations with Mirambo. The Governor of Tabora, Said ibn Salim, had been in office for many years, but during the long unsuccessful wars of the Arabs against Mirambo, his opponents accused him of aiding the latter. Whether the charge is true, or not, the Governor was driven from power by Abdullah ibn Nasib, who usurped his office.[38]

John Kirk was a determined enemy of Said ibn Salim because of the manner in which he had treated Livingstone,[39] but he also held no high opinion of Abdullah ibn Nasib,[40] and so he was ready to throw his considerable influence behind Mirambo in the hope that together they might keep the peace and protect the increasing number of European visitors to that part of East Africa. And then the news of Said ibn Salim's deposition, which occurred at either the end of 1877 or the beginning of 1878, reached him at the coast, along with the reports of Morton on Mirambo. For Morton had been much impressed by the African leader: to missionaries in the interior he described him as "a man of noble presence, of . great personal bravery, always leading his men in person, and exhibiting in his movements something of military talent." [41] Another missionary

37 Shergold Smith to Wright, 23. xi. 76, C. A6/0 22, C.M.S. Archives.
38 Norman R. Bennett, "The Arab Power of Tanganyika in the Nineteenth Century" (Boston University, Ph.D., 1961), 24–30.
39 See for example, Livingstone to Lord Stanley, 15. xi. 70, in *The New York Herald* of 17. viii. 72.
40 Bennett, "The Arab Power of Tanganyika," 26.
41 O'Neill to Wright, ?. x. 77, C. A6/0 18, C.M.S. Archives. O'Neill added: "You will be surprised to hear that he fights under the American flag which he captured from Stanley."

added: "Mirambo has offered to make a treaty with the Arabs, on honourable terms, provided they will pay him a tribute as a recognition of his power and status," [42] an offer which was refused. This and other accounts represented the future of the Nyamwezi region as very dark,[43] and, consequently, Kirk was all the more disposed to seek Mirambo's aid to secure peace. At this point, too, Mirambo fortified Kirk's favorable impression of him by offering to punish those Africans responsible for the death of two members of the C.M.S. in the region of Lake Victoria.[44]

So it was that when Morton prepared to return to the interior with the proceeds of the sale of Mirambo's ivory, Kirk entrusted him with a friendly message to the latter. The letter did not contain specific proposals; Kirk merely said that he concurred in his desire to "cement the friendship that exists between the people of the interior and the authorities at the coast and especially to open relations with the British agency and the Government of the Queen of Great Britain." Kirk apparently planned to add a few words about the Arabs, but in the end he deleted this passage from the draft of his message: "Now I have to caution you not to believe all the tales that are brought to you through the Arabs for they have many intrigues and it is their object to cause differences between the people of the country." [45] Kirk, after all, was accredited to the Arab government of Zanzibar and such a statement, if it became known, could cause much ill-feeling.

Now Mirambo had asked for more than this polite reply; he had urged that someone "be sent to help and advise him" and had offered "every assistance in his power to whoever may be sent to teach his people." [46] But Kirk was obviously feeling his way; he was seeking more information on this distant chief before making any firm commitment; in addition, he had to see what the Foreign Office thought about his moves. Fortunately, when his home authorities received his reports they supported his actions,[47] although notes on a Kirk dispatch referring to a desire of Mutesa of Buganda to open relations with the British government during

[42] Wilson to Wright, 8. ii. 78, C. A6/0 25, *ibid.*
[43] Bennett, "Arab Power of Tanganyika," 27 ff.
[44] E. Stock, *History of the Church Missionary Society* (London, 1899), III, 104, for details of this incident.
[45] Kirk to Derby, 6. iii. 78, enclosing Sayyid Barghash to Mirambo, 15. ii. 78, F.O. 84/1514; Kirk to Mirambo, 2. vii. 78 and Morton to Kirk, 18. vii. 78, N–25, Z.A. Needless to say, the Arabs were not pleased with this policy; see Kirk to Salisbury, 14. x. 78, F.O. 84/1515.
[46] Kirk to Derby, 3. v. 78, *ibid.*
[47] Pauncefote to Kirk, 31. v. 78, Q–19, Z.A.

this period show no overwhelming desire to extend British influence to African rulers. One official noted that dealings with Mutesa would encourage British trading interests and could be valuable if ever a Cape-to-Cairo telegraph line was built. Lord Salisbury, being not much impressed with this reasoning, observed: "unnecessary relations on the part of our Govt. with pure barbarians seldom end well," and backed his argument by recalling the difficulties the British had had in Abyssinia.[48] However, Kirk was left free to follow his policy to Mirambo.

Unfortunately for Kirk's schemes and for some later travellers to Mirambo, Morton was unable to accomplish his mission, for shortly after leaving the coast he contracted fever and shot himself in a fit of depression. The remains of the caravan returned to the coast, most of the proceeds of Mirambo's ivory being lost.[49]

Meantime, a new group of Europeans entered into relations with Mirambo and laid the foundations for long and intimate contact. The first London Missionary Society party proceeding to Ujiji on Lake Tanganyika, led by the Rev. J. B. Thomson, arrived in Urambo in July, 1878. The missionaries had heard much about Mirambo and decided to visit him to find out whether they could set up a mission establishment in his capital. As they travelled inland, they had written ahead, on the suggestion of the Swiss trader, Broyon, for aid in moving their goods, and Mirambo had replied in a very courteous manner.[50]

The missionaries were much impressed with Mirambo. He made no undue exactions upon them and readily agreed to aid them on their way to Ujiji, although he was not sanguine of their success there, because "the Arabs had been too long among them." So solicitous of them was he that he gave orders that anyone abusing them or their property would be executed. They feared this order might be carried out, and, indeed, later reports showed that Mirambo did execute a youth with his own hands for violating his command.[51] But the missionaries did not know this at the time, and sent good reports of him to their London directors. One of their accounts, that of E. C. Hore, gave this favorable description of Mirambo: "He is strictly temperate and actively engaged, so far as I can

---

48 Notes on Kirk to F.O., 17. viii. 78, F.O. 84/1515.

49 Bennett, "Broyon."

50 Thomson to Mullens, 5. iv. 78, L.M.S. Archives. Mullens later reported that Stanley, on his return from crossing Africa, had counseled the Society to visit Mirambo; see Mullens to Steere, 10. i. 79, *ibid.*

51 Edward Coode Hore, *Tanganyika* (London, 1892), 51 ff; Dawson, *Hannington*, 276.

see, in trying to establish a nationality and promote the progress and improvement of his people." To do this, said Hore, he wanted foreign residents, and thus was ready to receive a missionary or any other European at the court — "regarding them I fancy, just as a people who brought good things into his country." [52]

Mirambo also took advantage of this visit to seek a solution of some of his political difficulties, for his quarrels with the Tabora Arabs had revived in full force, the new Governor of Tabora being the object of his particular detestation. Mirambo had not only given asylum to the deposed Governor, Said ibn Salim, but was trying to restore him to office. Thus he requested the missionaries to tell Kirk when they returned to Zanzibar that Abdullah ibn Nasib had written to him to expel all Europeans. Mirambo urged them, too, to stress his own value to Europeans in keeping the trade routes of the interior open — the exact role Kirk wished him to play. Finally, Mirambo asked that Kirk use his influence to prevent Mutesa of Buganda from allying himself with the Arabs against him, there being rumors of such an arrangement.[53]

Thomson's party left but Mirambo was not to be for long without European visitors. In September, 1878, Lt. Cambier, leading the first expedition of the *Association Internationale Africaine* to go inland in East Africa, reached Urambo. Cambier wanted to investigate the feasibility of having his organization found a station there. He also wanted aid, for many of his men had deserted on the journey inland, leaving him in a very precarious position. Mirambo gave him a ready welcome, made blood-brotherhood with him, and promised to recruit porters from his people. Then, however, began three difficult months. Mirambo extracted presents, especially firearms, from the hapless Belgian, and in spite of repeated promises did not supply the needed porters. Part of the delay was due to a campaign by Mirambo in Usukuma, but this did not excuse his actions. Cambier, understandably, soon became entirely disenchanted with the chief and looked for the first opportunity to leave with his remaining possessions.[54]

[52] Hore to Mullens, 4. viii. 78, L.M.S. Archives; Thomson to Mullens, 4. viii. 78, *ibid.* Mirambo's rejection of liquor particularly impressed the missionaries — he explained it in this way to a later mission visitor: "I could not do all my business and govern my people well if I drank pombe." See Dawson, *Hannington,* 275.

[53] Thomson to Kirk, 3. viii. 78 and –. viii. 78, in Kirk to Salisbury, 18. ix. 78, F.O. 84/1515. Kirk claimed here full credit for blocking any Arab-Mutesa alliance. Distance alone, however, would have made this impossible.

[54] *Association Internationale Africaine. Comité National Belge. Séance Publique du 1er Mars 1881* (Bruxelles, 1880), 17; Burdo, *Tanganika,* 28 ff. According to

In the midst of his troubles, Cambier received letters from some Belgian compatriots who were advancing inland with a new caravan. The party, which included two Belgians (one of them died *en route*), and a L.M.S. missionary, was directed by Broyon who was returning goods to Mirambo for ivory sold in Zanzibar, and in addition executing a contract to deliver supplies to the L.M.S. in Ujiji. Unfortunately for the party's prospects, a C.M.S. lay missionary, Penrose, travelling ahead of them, was killed through no fault of his own by an African band. When the Belgians with Broyon heard from Cambier in response to their communications to him, not only of the treatment he was receiving at the hands of Mirambo, but also that Mirambo was allegedly responsible for Penrose's death, they began to have trouble with their porters, who took fright at the news and threatened to desert unless the course was altered. Accordingly, Broyon changed the caravans' route and bypassed Urambo, going straight to Tabora.[55]

Broyon and his party reached Uyui, near both Urambo and Tabora, but could proceed no farther since their porters at that point refused to go on. So Broyon went ahead alone to Tabora to secure new men. But Uyui, as it happened, was the headquarters of Said ibn Salim, and he wrote to Mirambo of this affair. The latter took action at once to protect the proceeds from the sale of his ivory by seizing the Swiss trader's goods, including those he was carrying for the L.M.S. The Europeans were not harmed, and they, with Cambier, went on to Tabora. Mutual mistrust prevented any settlement, although Mirambo did offer to return the goods of the L.M.S. if a representative came to Urambo. In the end the Europeans at Tabora went their various ways and the merchandise was left in Urambo with Mirambo.[56]

These events did not shake Kirk's confidence in Mirambo as an ally in stabilizing this area of Africa. He absolved him of any connection with the death of Penrose, even though it was caused by an associate of his, and went so far as to condone his action in seizing Broyon's property. For Kirk felt that Mirambo had reason to act, since Broyon, who did owe him merchandise, had tried to divert his caravan to Tabora, the center of Arabs hostile to him. This judgment was probably correct, but Kirk

---

Burdo's information, Mirambo told Cambier there were only three kinds of Europeans: the English who always supported him, the Americans who allied with the Arabs, and the French — the rest.

[55] Bennett, "Broyon."
[56] *Ibid.*

was overly hard on the Europeans. They had, after all, been forced to act on the basis of the information available to them in the interior — all unfavorable to Mirambo — and they had to control their potentially mutinous porters. Kirk, however, was firm in his convictions and never made allowances, thereby securing for Broyon Mirambo's continued hostility [57] and ruining the career of the Swiss as an African trader.

Kirk could maintain this attitude to Mirambo because a new European visitor had just been welcomed in Urambo: E. J. Southon of the L.M.S., who arrived there in August, 1879, to establish a permanent mission station. In spite of a friendly reception, Southon was a little suspicious at first. He said:

> My first impressions of Mirambo were decidedly of an unpleasant nature. He appeared as simply a bandit chief and . . . he stood surrounded by his fierce-looking men, clad for the most part in stolen goods [from the L.M.S.'s property!], and all excited as . . . with wine . . . His face showed a careless abandon and his frequent jokes to his excited followers told, I thought, of either a suppressed anxiety or exultation.

Southon soon changed his opinions. Mirambo warmed to him, won over by the successful removal of a cyst from his arm, and promised full support for the establishment of a mission station. Mirambo's attitude to the new venture is best inferred from a statement of Southon's concerning his intellectual curiosity: "He handles a new thing as thoughtfully as a skilled mechanic would a piece of beautiful mechanism, the working of which he does not yet understand." [58]

Mirambo, naturally, lost no time in trying to use Southon in his efforts to gain more active support from Kirk. He dictated a letter to Southon for the Consul complaining that Kirk had as yet answered his earlier letters only in a general way and he went on to say that if Abdullah ibn Nasib remained Governor of Tabora at the end of the rainy season, war would result. An implicit threat accompanied the last statement: "tell him that I won't be responsible for any caravans being attacked, the road will be closed and if white men or Arabs get killed, don't blame me."

---

[57] Mirambo's first biographer upheld Kirk's view of this affair. He said: "There is no shred of evidence to connect him [Mirambo] with this tragic incident . . ." See Harvey, "Mirambo," 17. This judgment disregards the letters of Cambier based on the information he gained in Urambo.

[58] Southon's "Journal," entry of 30. viii. 79 and Southon to L.M.S., 16. vii. 79, L.M.S. Archives.

Then Mirambo passed on to the subject of Said ibn Salim, for Kirk had been trying to tempt Said back to the coast with a promise of asylum, and Said, himself now ill, had requested Southon to intercede with Mirambo to this end. But Mirambo refused them both, saying: "I want him to be Governor of Unyanyembe [Tabora], for he is a good man and wants to live in peace with everyone." [59]

Kirk was anxious to prevent war — his offer of asylum to Said proved this — but there was little he could do. Abdullah ibn Nasib ruled in Tabora, and the Sultan of Zanzibar lacked the power to remove him. Kirk might oppose him and wish for a better man, one who would "work with the native chiefs, the actual rulers of the country," but he could go no farther than the Sultan. Southon tried to explain all this to Mirambo. He probably did not succeed in convincing him, and what actually eased the situation was the death of the unfortunate Said ibn Salim. [60]

In March, 1880, the Sultan appeared to be seeking an end to interior disorder through negotiation. His messengers arrived at Tabora inquiring about Abdullah ibn Nasib's grievances against Mirambo; next, they did the same with Mirambo. The Sultan's agent, however, became ill and another man went to Urambo. Mirambo did not trust him and sent his own representatives to Tabora. The Arab delegate spent most of his time speaking against the English, warning Mirambo that they would eventually take over his country and prevent him from taking slaves in his numerous wars. [61] Nothing resulted from these negotiations.

All this time, throughout the years 1879 and 1880, Mirambo was very busy expanding his influence. In 1879, he campaigned in Uvinza and successfully blocked the normal trade route from there to the coast. At one moment this venture threw the Ujiji Arabs into panic — they thought he was about to raid them — but all passed peacefully. Mirambo said later he did not attack Ujiji since his English missionary friends of the L.M.S. were living there. [62] But the warlike activity, continuing in 1880, ultimately cost Mirambo the support of Kirk. The Nyamwezi leader, extending operations, led a large war party to fight an enemy in the area south of the Ugala River. When the latter fled, Mirambo changed his

[59] Southon's "Journal," entry of 6. ix. 79, *ibid.*; Southon to Kirk, 9. ix. 79, K–1, Z.A.
[60] Kirk to F.O., 31. v. 79 and 15. x. 79, Q–22, *ibid.*; Southon to L.M.S., 24. xii. 79, L.M.S. Archives.
[61] Southon's "Journal," entry of 29. iii. 80 and Southon to L.M.S., 28. iii. 80, *ibid.*
[62] Kirk to F.O., 7. xi. 79, enclosing Hore to Kirk, 15. x. 79 and 27. v. 79, and 27. v. 79, Q–22, Z.A.; Hore to Guiness, 10. xii. 79, *The Regions Beyond,* (June 1880), 19.

plan of campaign and joined with the ruler of the African village of Konongo, Simba, to attack another African leader, Kasogera of Mpimbwe.[63]

While these events were taking place, an expedition of Leopold II of
Belgium entered the area of operations, led by two Englishmen, Carter
and Cadenhead. They were returning to the coast from Karema, the *Association*'s station on Lake Tanganyika, to prepare for the arrival of some
Indian elephants, for Carter, who had earlier attempted to lead four Indian elephants from the coast to Karema, all of whom eventually died,
was, nonetheless, convinced of their usefulness as beasts of burden in Africa. The Englishmen decided to try a different route to the coast to
avoid certain African chiefs who charged a heavy *hongo* (payment) for
passing through their territories. They were warned of the unsettled nature of the country through which they planned to pass, but they took
the chance and went ahead since, after all, all travel in the East Africa of
that era had its dangers.[64]

Carter and Cadenhead arrived at Kasogera's village of Mpimbwe in
June, 1880, just when the allied forces of Simba and Mirambo were mo-
mentarily expected to attack. Kasogera invited them into the village, but
Carter declined this: he said that they had no interest in local quarrels
and planned to leave in the morning. Kasogera replied that if they did
not come into Mpimbwe he would consider them as allies of Mirambo
and attack. He was inclined to suspect them, in any case, because of the
fact that they had arrived at the same time as Mirambo. Carter thereupon called a council of his men who maintained that it would be folly to
disobey and recommended compliance with Kasogera's wishes. Carter
hesitated but when hostile demonstrations started around them, he gave
in and entered the village.

Mirambo's and Simba's forces then attacked the village. The Englishmen collected their followers and attempted to prove their neutrality to
the invading forces, but, eventually, one party of invaders opened fire on
them. Cadenhead was killed at once, and after brief resistance, Carter
died fighting. Most of the Africans in the English caravan broke and fled
while the fighting was yet in progress.[65]

Tidings of the disaster first reached the various Europeans in East Africa when the refugees from Carter's group arrived at their respective

  [63] Harvey, "Mirambo," 18.
  [64] Burdo, *Tanganika*, 336 ff.
  [65] Carter's "Journal," entries of 12–24. vi. 80, Storms Papers, Musée Royale de
l'Afrique Centrale, Tervuren, Belgium.

places of residence. A vehement disagreement ensued at once over the question of Mirambo's responsibility for the affair: Did he know the Englishmen were in Mpimbwe? Did he actually order their death? Did he learn of the tragedy too late to take any action?

The Belgians, who probably received the news first, concluded at once that Mirambo was clearly implicated in the death of the Englishmen. They picked up the story that Mirambo knew Carter and his group were there when he attacked and were convinced that Mirambo had actually given the order to fire on them, or his men would never have moved against Europeans. In the light of this, Capt. Popelin, our chief informant on the subject, requested the Sultan of Zanzibar to take steps to punish Mirambo.[66]

A differing view came from Southon at Urambo. He reported that Mirambo gave him full liberty to investigate the tragedy on his return from Mpimbwe and that he had learned the "true facts" of the situation, namely, that Mirambo had no idea that Europeans were in the village until their bodies were discovered when the fighting was over and that he had shown "the utmost concern," exclaiming in dismay, "Just as I was beginning to be believed by the white men, this has happened, which will make them believe I am their enemy." Southon concluded with the hope that no retaliatory action would be taken by the authorities at Zanzibar since that would probably ruin the prospects of his mission.[67]

The most influential opinion regarding Mirambo's responsibility was that of John Kirk, the British Consul. His first report of the affair was hostile: that the African leader had been waging war to gain control of trade routes which did not pass through his territory; that Carter, knowing this, had tried to find a route that would bypass Mirambo and his army. To Kirk, "this however was exactly what Mirambo had set himself to stop," and so the attack took place. Kirk was all the more upset since this new campaign of Mirambo's was undertaken in spite of all his advice to the contrary; he also thought that Mirambo had taken advantage of his

[66] Popelin à Sultan de Zanzibar, 11. viii. 80, in Kirk to F.O., 18. x. 80, Q–24, N–6, Z.A.; Popelin à Kirk, 17. viii. 80, K–1, *ibid.;* Strauch à Ramaeckers, 19. xi. 80, Storms Papers; *Mittheilungen der Afrikanischen Gesellschaft in Deutschland,* II (1880–81), 212. Cambier, however, said that Mirambo seemed strongly against what his men had done; see Cambier à Kirk, 18. vii. 80, N–6, Z.A.

[67] Southon to Kirk, 13. viii. 80, K–1, *ibid.;* Southon to L.M.S., 13. viii. 80 and 14. ix. 80, L.M.S. Archives. Other missionaries supported Southon's interpretation; see Stokes to Kirk, received 21. x. 80, K–1, Z.A., for an example. Stokes had reversed an earlier hostile attitude to Mirambo on receiving more information; his original views were in Stokes to Kirk, 5. ix. 80, N–6, *ibid.*

efforts to keep the Tabora Arabs at peace.[68] Later information merely confirmed Kirk in his views, for in September he learned from new sources that Mirambo had spies watching the village the day before the attack, and thus must have known of the Europeans. Hence there was no doubt in his mind that Mirambo was directly responsible for the deaths of Carter and Cadenhead.[69]

Kirk's views took on special significance when the Sultan of Zanzibar, always much under his influence,[70] began to prepare a military expedition for work in the interior. Kirk said little of this expedition at first, but he did report home that the Arabs considered Mirambo's actions to be a declaration of war against them, and that the Sultan would move to occupy the important caravan station of Mpwapwa. Kirk therefore wrote Southon at Urambo: "[my] advice he has now deliberately rejected and taking advantage of the opportunities given him by my intervention has attacked villages far from his borders for the obvious purpose of eventually crushing the independent native tribes in alliance with or likely to be friendly to the Zanzibar traders of Unyanyembe." He warned Southon that he should evacuate his station since the Sultan would have no control over events in the interior if the Tabora Arabs now began hostilities.[71] Southon replied that both his "duty and inclination" as a missionary prevented him from leaving and that he planned to stay to use his influence with Mirambo to maintain peace.[72]

The home authorities of the British missionary societies established in the interior of East Africa reacted strongly to this talk of war. Both the C.M.S. and the L.M.S. approached the Foreign Office to make known their objection to any military ventures by the Sultan — and Kirk. They called for an investigation to precede any such move; after all, had not Mirambo's past record been one of friendship with Europeans? A joint memorial was sent by the two missionary societies to the Foreign Office, protesting against any untoward action since

[68] Kirk to F.O., 20. viii. 80, Q–24, *ibid.*
[69] Kirk to F.O., 21. ix. 80, *ibid.*
[70] A Swahili saying described the relationship of Kirk to the Sultan in these terms: *"anakata maneno sote"* — "he decides all the cases" — given in Paul Reichard, *Deutsch-Ostafrika* (Leipzig, 1892), 12.
[71] Kirk to F.O., 24. viii. 80, Q–24, Z.A.; Kirk to Southon, 12. viii. 80, in Southon to L.M.S., 29. xi. 80, L.M.S. Archives.
[72] Southon to L.M.S., 29. vi. 80, *ibid.;* Southon to Kirk, 29. xi. 80, in Kirk to F.O., 12. vi. 81, Q–25, Z.A.; Southon to Kirk, 1. i. 81, in Kirk to F.O., 8. iii. 81, *ibid.*

The maintenance of friendly relations with this chief Mirambo appears to be of much importance and to the highest interest of the natives of the country and also to the development and opening up of the interior to legitimate trade and the introduction of civilisation.

The memorial concluded: "any hostile movement of the Sultan of Zanzibar against Mirambo . . . is unjust and uncalled-for and likely to lead to the most disastrous results." [73]

When these documents were forwarded to Kirk, he denied warmly that he had ever even hinted that an expedition was planned against Mirambo as punishment for the Carter affair; rather, it was the Sultan, who, even before this sad event, had plans for a line of stations in the interior to protect his interests; but this policy did not envisage any fighting, as the missionaries claimed. The only reason for his warning the missionaries, Kirk said, was that a party of Belgians had sped inland when they learned of Carter's death, a step that could have produced trouble. Kirk concluded by protesting that the only act yet taken by the Sultan against Mirambo was to prevent gunpowder from reaching him from the coast.[74]

Kirk's explanations do not entirely agree with other information from East Africa. Two expeditions had gone inland, as he stated. The first, the latest group of Belgians to arrive in Zanzibar, was ordered inland at once to protect their remaining compatriots; it received minor aid from the Sultan.[75] The second was a purely Zanzibari affair that does not fit Kirk's reports: the French Consul reported a party of two hundred and fifty men was preparing to go inland in the face of the Sultan's objection that the costs were very heavy. Once this group did get underway, frequent desertions, following news of possible hostilities with Mirambo, prevented any successful conclusion. As a matter of fact, on this point all information is unclear; a Belgian reporter agreed with Kirk in calling this a fort-building party, while a French resident of Zanzibar said its purpose was to pacify the interior. And the Belgian Consul noted facts unmentioned by Kirk: that the Sultan had offered a reward of 50,000 francs for Mirambo and that Kirk had openly disavowed Southon at

[73] Hutchinson to Granville, 18. ix. 80, in Lister to Kirk, 24. ix. 80, Q–23, *ibid.;* Hutchinson to Granville, 15. i. 81, in Lister to Kirk, 8. ii. 81, N–24, *ibid.*

[74] Note by Kirk on Lister to Kirk, 8. ii. 81, *ibid.;* Kirk to F.O., 8. iii. 81, Q–25, *ibid.*

[75] Ledoulx à M.A.E., 14. viii. 80, Correspondance Commercial, Zanzibar, t. 4 bis, Ministère des Affaires Étrangères, Paris.

Urambo because of his pro-Mirambo attitude.[76] Thus it appears likely
that Kirk encouraged the Sultan to take forceful action against Mirambo
but that when news of it reached London, he denied it and let the scheme
drop. The inference is credible, the more so because the non-British
observers specified all too many events that the usually observant Kirk
should have reported home. In any event, there were so many rumors
concerning expeditions that the attitude of the missionary societies was
certainly justified.[77]

After the missionaries' protest, Kirk was careful to demonstrate that his
antagonism to Mirambo was justified, and in this, new information from
the interior helped him. Hore of the L.M.S., in conversation with Mirambo, learned that the African leader had strong feelings against the Belgians. Their occupation of Karema was a sore point with him; he complained that Cambier had received his "hospitality" and then went on
"to his town of Karema . . . [to] build without asking his permission, or
even communicating in any way to him their intentions." [78] This, to Kirk,
confirmed his views; here was Mirambo making claims to territory not
previously under his influence. Therefore, Kirk concluded, it was impossible for him to work any longer with Mirambo:

> To me, I may say, it is a sad disappointment to give up the hope that under
> good advice Mirambo might be content to raise and extend his influence in
> a more legitimate way for the power and prestige his name now carries with
> it would have been of incalculable service.

To Southon Kirk said: "I still hold to supporting native states and chiefs,
but Mirambo, in his present power, seems a dangerous man and likely to
do more harm than good." [79]

Kirk still had a plan for Mirambo in the interior. He suggested that

[76] Ledoulx à M.A.E., 7. ix. 80 and 11. xi. 80, Politique, Zanzibar, t. 5, Ministère
des Affaires Étrangères, Paris; Greffuhle à Popelin, 12. viii. 80, Storms Papers; de Ville
à Lambermont, 24. viii. 80, Correspondance et Documents. Afrique. A.I.A. 1876–
1884, Ministère des Affaires Étrangères, Bruxelles; Burdo, *Les Arabs dan l'Afrique
Centrale*, 19–20. A later report confirmed the French statement of the Consul's suspicions of Southon. Orders were given to check supplies sent to him to see if they
contained gunpowder for Mirambo; see Hore to L.M.S., 27. ix. 82, L.M.S. Archives.

[77] For these rumors as reported from the interior, Southon's "Journal," entry of
10. xi. 80, L.M.S. Archives and Copplestone to Hutchinson, 27. x. 80, G3. A6/0 1,
C.M.S. Archives.

[78] This quarrel with the Belgians will be discussed below.

[79] Kirk to Granville, 21. i. 81, *Slave Trade Correspondence presented to Parlia-
ment in 1881*, Z.A.; Kirk to F.O., 14. xi. 80, Q–24, Z.A.; Southon to L.M.S., 1. i. 81,
L.M.S. Archives.

the Sultan be informed his "dominions" beyond Tabora really belonged to the independent Mirambo. The Sultan then could concentrate on making his own territory secure, while maintaining the gunpowder blockade against Mirambo, and in the end they might work together for their mutual benefit and the stability of the area. But the Foreign Office did not support this reasoning; instead, Kirk was instructed "to avoid committing Her Majesty's Government to any policy entailing a definition of the extent of the Sultan's territory inland." [80] Thus peace depended upon Kirk's interpretation as to how he should deal with Mirambo. As will appear, he never reversed his attitude towards him.

In retrospect, which view was the more correct? Kirk's and the Belgians'? or Southon's? Recent students conclude that Mirambo was not directly responsible for the murders, which they blame on the difficulty in controlling men in the heat of battle.[81] This view cannot be entirely accepted. As Hore's conversation with Mirambo revealed and as events to be discussed below will confirm, the chief was very hostile to the Belgians. Kirk and the Belgians offer sufficient proof that Mirambo was aware of who was in Mpimbwe. Yet this does not mean that Southon was entirely wrong; he said Mirambo showed much regret when the bodies were found — possibly because he learned only then that he had been responsible for the death, not of two Belgians, but of two Englishmen working for Leopold II. In summary, the present writer believes that Mirambo must bear full responsibility for a grievous miscalculation that lost him the support of the British in Zanzibar.

Mirambo was greatly upset by this turn of events, especially because of the powder blockade maintained against him on the coast. He sent down a party to trade soon after the difficulties at Mpimbwe, probably to test Kirk, and found the latter persisting in his attitude. His men were left to their own devices, and being unfamiliar with the mechanics of trade and the wiles of the Indian merchants of Zanzibar, they were roundly victimized.[82] Thus Mirambo had to face the fact that no plans of his for central Tanganyika would get aid from Zanzibar.

[80] Lister to Kirk, 18. iv. 81, N–24, Z.A.; R. Coupland, *The Exploitation of East Africa, 1856–1890* (London, 1939), 265–66.
[81] Smith, "Historical Introduction," *Maisha ya . . . Tippu Tip,* 19; Harvey, "Mirambo," 19.
[82] Stokes to Hutchinson, 20. x. 80, G3. A6/0 1, C.M.S. Archives; Southon's "Journal," entries of 12 and 21. viii. 80, L.M.S. Archives; Southon to Kirk, 13. viii. 80, K–1, Z.A. Mirambo, however, was able to get some powder originating from Portuguese territory; see Kirk to F.O., 11. xii. 80, Q–24, Z.A.

III

The year 1881 was an active one for Mirambo; he continued his campaigning, but only against Africans; the Arabs of Tabora he left in peace. He told Southon in December, 1880, that the Tabora Arabs had said they would not fight him, a promise they kept, and he himself made no moves to cause them to regret it.[83]   In a campaign, which he started at the end of that month, against the Ugala River area, and particularly the African center of Ugunda,[84] a village that had earlier repulsed his forces, his men were very active, but, deterred, perhaps by the Arab influence in Ugunda, he made no serious effort against the village.   This campaign led to minor difficulties with another European group, the German section of the *Association*, the *Afrikanischen Gesellschaft in Deutschland*, which had representatives in the region.   They withdrew to a position of safety during the native hostilities, but Mirambo's men visited them, made an "impudent demand" for tribute, and then left with no result but to have increased the Europeans' ill-will toward Mirambo.   Mirambo later disavowed the incident.[85]

In 1881, Mirambo again occupied himself in the region between Urambo and Lake Victoria.   In March, Southon reported that the African leader had returned from a campaign that had taken him to the shores of Lake Victoria.   The extent of his control there was tested when he promised a party of C.M.S. men that they would not have to pay *hongo* while passing through on their way to Victoria, and they found that his commands were obeyed.   They noted that his dominions ended at the village of Msalala on the Lake, the original home of one of his wives.   In this campaign Mirambo brought many other villages under his influence and exchanged presents with Mutesa of Buganda in an attempt to gain support for his military plans there.[86]   He tried, too, to use the opportunity his predominance gave him in this region to aid missionaries, in an effort to regain Kirk's support.   As he told one missionary: "Now . . . you will write and tell your big people that Mirambo the robber is changed, and he has now a peaceful country." [87]   But the effort was fruitless.

[83] Southon to L.M.S., 31. xii. 80. L.M.S. Archives.
[84] For a report on Ugunda, Norman R. Bennett, "Captain Storms in Tanganyika: 1882–1885," *Tanganyika Notes and Records*, 54 (1960), 55–6.
[85] R. Böhm, *Von Sansibar zum Tanganjika* (Leipzig, 1888), 55, 85–8.
[86] Kirk to F.O., 29. vii. 81, Q–25, Z.A.; Copplestone's "Journal," entry of 28. iv. 81, G3. A6/0 1, C.M.S. Archives; Stokes to C.M.S., 8. xii. 81, *ibid.;* Dawson, *Hannington,* 238.
[87] Stokes to Lang, 9. xi. 82, G3. A6/0 1, C.M.S. Archives.

Though his truce with the Arabs continued, Mirambo wanted a more formal arrangement, and sent delegates to the Sultan of Zanzibar for the purpose,[88] but little progress was made. He also tried negotiations when his erstwhile allies, the Ngoni, sought Arab support in a quarrel they had with him. Both he and the Ngoni sent delegations carrying gifts to Tabora. Though Mirambo gave the largest gift, he secured no promises of aid. But the Ngoni fared even worse: the Arabs told them to return home since their gift was too small.[89]

In that year, too, Mirambo became involved indirectly in missionary intrigues. Southon, who enjoyed undisputed influence with him, heard that Roman Catholics were thinking of entering into closer relations with the chief, and that Mirambo approved their activities. Southon then explained to the Nyamwezi leader that Roman Catholics were the "avowed enemies" of his mission and he succeeded in extracting the promise that only the English Protestants should be represented at his capital.[90] It should be noted, incidentally, that Southon and his aides were making little apparent progress in their missionary endeavors at Urambo. Mirambo never gave any real sign of a desire for conversion, and his people followed his lead. In fact, when one of the missionaries asked Mirambo if he knew why they were there, he replied that he did not, and asked, rather plaintively, "why was it that God had told and given so many things to the English people and not to black men?"[91]

By 1882 Mirambo was extremely dissatisfied with the character of his relations with Kirk and the Sultan of Zanzibar. The Nyamwezi chief of Tabora, instigated by the Arabs, was raising difficulties for him in Usukuma, and the continuing powder blockade presented a serious obstacle to his plans for expansion since it did not extend to chiefs in opposition to him. In an attempt to rescue himself from the impasse, Mirambo asked Southon to write to the then British representative, Col. Miles:

> Tell the British Consul I only ask a more rigid investigation of my affairs in connection with other tribes around me and in the interest of trade I would respectfully ask that he would send some responsible agent from his office to dictate the line of policy I should pursue towards others at the same time giving me his help and support in carrying these out. I am aware that the

[88] Ledoulx à M.A.E., 5. iv. 81, Corr. Comm., Zanz., t. 4 bis; Southon to L.M.S., 23. ii. 81, L.M.S. Archives.

[89] Jerome Becker, *La Troisième Expédition Belge* (Bruxelles, n.d.), 213–14.

[90] Southon to L.M.S., 15. viii. 81, L.M.S. Archives.

[91] D. Williams, "Journal," entry of 4. i. 81, *ibid.* Compare with Wilhelm Blohm, *Die Nyamwezi* (Hamburg, 1933), 141.

constant fighting I am compelled to do is displeasing to him, but I am really
trying to reduce this to a minimum and I hope soon to live at peace with all
around me.

Mirambo went on to observe that the small chiefs of his area needed a
strong hand to keep them in order and that providing it would serve the
best interests of trade. He complained that a recent embassy he had sent
to Zanzibar had been denied a hearing by the Sultan — his present had
even been refused — and the British Consul treated his men in the same
way. Mirambo concluded: "I wish to open it [my country] up, to learn
of Europeans, to trade honestly with all and to cultivate peaceful relationships with my neighbors." [92] Southon added his support to this plea,
but, perhaps unwisely, the authorities in Zanzibar saw no reason to mod-
ify their attitude to Mirambo.

Yet in spite of his lack of success with the Tabora Arabs and the Zanzibar authorities, Mirambo did succeed in establishing satisfactory relations with the leading Arab of Central Africa, Tippu Tip. In mid-1882,
when Tippu Tip was *en route* to the coast with a very large caravan laden
with the fruits of a long stay in the interior, Mirambo carefully kept his
forces in hand so that no compromising incidents could occur. This was
particularly important since Tippu Tip had to fight his way through
Uvinza: an African had committed a minor theft from his caravan, and re-
prisals led to general fighting. The chief of those warring with Tippu Tip
later came to Mirambo seeking alliance against the trader, but Mirambo
turned him down.

It appears that once Tippu Tip reached Tabora, Mirambo sent representatives to him to negotiate peace and an outlet to the coast for his
ivory, objectives he thought Tippu Tip might possibly accomplish for
him. Beside that, the African leader had to make sure that the Tabora
Arabs did not win the powerful Tippu Tip to their side. [93] Following
Mirambo's initiative, Tippu Tip sent a group of his men to visit Urambo.
They were treated extremely well and returned to report Mirambo's re-
fusal to join their enemy, the Vinza. With this encouragement, the Arab
trader sent his son, Sefu, to Urambo for more serious negotiations, a step
which provoked the Tabora Arabs, for Tippu Tip, after all, was an out-

    [92] Southon to L.M.S., 25. iii. 82, *ibid.*
    [93] Brode, *Tippoo Tib*, 14, 151–52; *Maisha ya . . . Tippu Tip*, 131, 135, 125, 17;
Hermann Wissmann, *Unter deutscher Flagge quer durch Afrika von West nach Ost*
(Berlin, 1889), 239.

sider stepping in to arrange a peace that they never had been able to conclude; he might then profit accordingly.

Thereupon, the Tabora Arabs launched a program of intrigue. After Sefu arrived in Urambo, they sent ten Nyamwezis, dressed as if they had just returned from the coast, to report that a large force from the Sultan of Zanzibar was on its way inland to take action against Mirambo. The Tabora traders apparently hoped that this ruse would cause Mirambo either to kill Sefu or hold him as a hostage. But Mirambo met this move very ably. He sent to Sefu and advised him to order the Arabs with him to leave Urambo since their men might panic and desert when they learned the news. Thus he succeeded in removing a potentially hostile body from his capital and also prevented any incidents from being precipitated by his excitable followers. Then, having dispatched men to investigate the truth of these rumors and learning that they were untrue, he gave Sefu gifts and allowed him to return to Tabora. He had, of course, been a potentially useful hostage up to this point. The outcome of it all was an agreement that Tippu Tip would use his influence in Zanzibar to establish Mirambo in the position he desired in the interior.[94]

We owe some of the above information to the German explorer, Hermann von Wissmann, who was present in Urambo at the time. The first German to visit Mirambo, he later made enthusiastic reports in Europe about the Nyamwezi chief, remarking that he was "charmed with Mirambo's manner" — and well he might be since Mirambo greeted him with two bottles of champagne! During their friendly meetings, Wissmann, who was to become leader of the German forces in the Arab-German war of 1888–90, made plans to return to Urambo for an expedition to the yet-undiscovered lake, Muta Nzige (Lake Albert Edward). Mirambo was to be supplied with powder, and, in addition, was to receive all the ivory secured on the trip.[95] This venture never materialized.

In Zanzibar, Tippu Tip was either unwilling or unable to accomplish

---

[94] *Ibid.*, 262–72; *Maisha ya . . . Tippu Tip*, 135, 137; Herbert Ward, *Five Years with the Congo Cannibals* (London, 1890), 186–88; Copplestone to L.M.S., 28. ix. 82, L.M.S. Archives. Von Wissmann claimed later he had prevented Mirambo from holding Sefu prisoner: Hermann von Wissmann, *My Second Journey Through Equatorial Africa* (London, 1891), 221, 225.

[95] Hermann Wissmann, "Von San Paúlo de Loanda nach Zanzibar," *Mittheilungen de Kais. und kön. Geographischen Gesellschaft*, XXV (1882), 97–105; Wissmann, *Unter deutscher Flagge*, 239 ff; Copplestone to L.M.S., 28. ix. 82, L.M.S. Archives. Harvey, "Mirambo," 22, is in error in saying another German explorer, Pogge, was with Wissmann; he left him at Nyangwe.

anything for Mirambo: the Tabora Arabs remained a threat and rumors of war were rife. The powder blockade continued. Wissmann had noticed its serious consequences for Mirambo; moreover, its effectiveness can be judged from reports of travellers near the Sultan's post of Mpwapwa, that the officials tried to check all caravans to see if they complied with the blockade, and that the Governor of Tabora had orders to sell no powder to any Nyamwezi for fear it might reach Mirambo.[96] But in spite of failure, relations between Mirambo and Tippu Tip remained cordial. On his return to Central Africa in early 1883, the Arab leader visited Mirambo for the first time, after requesting and receiving from him porters to aid him on his way. The Tabora Arabs, continuing their intrigues against their friendship, started rumors that Tippu Tip was coming to attack Mirambo, but to no purpose. Tippu Tip was very pleased at the meeting: "Great honour was accorded to me," he said, "and a great friendship was established." [97]

Mirambo could not hope for more mediation by Tippu Tip, but he still wished to attain better relations with the Arabs. He sent new missions to Zanzibar and was careful to let Arab caravans pass through his territories in peace. He had no success, however, even though one report mentions gifts to him sent by the Sultan in 1884.[98]

All the time that Mirambo was dealing with Tippu Tip in the interests of better relations with the Arabs, he continued to expand his influence to new regions. At the end of 1881 he went to war with his former ally against Kasogera, Simba of Konongo,[99] driving him from his village and then building a new fort to control the regional trade. In the course of these operations, his men began to threaten the region around the Belgian station of Karema. As already noted, this station was a vexation to Mirambo since he claimed the locality as his own. The Belgian officer in charge, Capt. Ramaeckers, had already been isolated for some time by the unsettled conditions and Mirambo's new venture understandably worried his fellow officers in Africa. Mirambo's men made the danger acute

---

[96] Wissmann, *Unter deutscher Flagge,* 258; Becker, *La Vie en Afrique,* II, 428; Hutley to L.M.S., 23. i. 82, L.M.S. Archives; Last to Lang, 25. v. 85, G3. A6/0 1, C.M.S Archives.

[97] *Maisha ya . . . Tippu Tip,* 143.

[98] Copplestone to Lang, 17. i. 83, G3. A6/0 1, C.M.S. Archives; Hore to L.M.S., 22. i. 83, L.M.S. Archives; Carnochan and Adamson, *Out of Africa,* 236.

[99] For Simba, see *Maisha ya . . . Tippu Tip,* 69. Later reports from Katanga speak of a raider, Simba, who might be the same man. See Edgard Verdick, *Les Premiers Jours au Katanga (1890–1903)* (Bruxelles, 1952), 67–9.

by visiting Ramaeckers to demand he pay tribute; he put them off and began preparations for future conflict.[100]

The Belgians naturally rejected Mirambo's claims to Karema, and on firm grounds, for when Cambier first went to the area he dealt with the Africans in control in reaching agreement for the land, and there were no signs then of Mirambo's authority.[101] The Belgians had to take action, nevertheless, to meet the new claim. They were willing to deal with him, thus letting pass the episode of Carter and Cadenhead, but there was little alternative. Their original plan was to have Ramaeckers visit Urambo to talk the situation over. He was to be careful to give no sign of recognition to Mirambo's claims to Karema. Carter and Cadenhead would not even be mentioned and the difficulties with Cambier would all be blamed on the unfortunate Swiss trader, Broyon. Finally, while the discussions were going on, Ramaeckers would establish close relation with Southon so that the missionary might aid them in the future.[102]

This scheme had to be changed when Ramaeckers died of dysentery in February, 1882.[103] Another Belgian officer then in East Africa took the initiative: Jerome Becker, representative of the *Association* in Tabora, slipped off to Urambo by a devious route to discuss the problem of Karema. Mirambo claimed that he knew nothing of the doings of his men there, and promised to punish the leaders of the guilty. Then after explaining his opposition to the Belgian establishment at Karema, Mirambo agreed to let them rule there with no payment of tribute to him. All this was accomplished by verbal agreement, Mirambo protesting that nothing more was necessary to bind him.[104]

This, although it stabilized the situation, was against the wishes of the leaders of the *Association*, for it implied that Mirambo actually did have rights in Karema. Strauch of the *Association* had written Ramaeckers earlier that Becker did not have the temperament for negotiation [105] and his agreement with Mirambo was certainly not pleasing; in fact, at the very time of Becker's negotiations, Strauch was instructing Ramaeckers'

[100] Ledoulx à M.A.E., 25. viii. 81, 12. i. 82, 8. ii. 82, 8. iii. 82, Corr. Comm., Zanz., t. 4 bis; Ramaeckers à Strauch, 31. i. 82, Storms Papers; *Bulletin de la Société de Géographie d'Anvers*, VII (1882), 76; Becker, *La Vie en Afrique*, II, 78 ff.

[101] Burdo, *Tanganika*, 54 ff.

[102] Strauch à Ramaeckers, 10. ii. 82 and 7. iv. 82, Storms Papers.

[103] Ledoulx à M.A.E., 4. v. 82, Corr. Comm. Zanz., t. 4 bis.

[104] Becker, *La Vie en Afrique*, II, 151 ff; Burdo, *Tanganika*, 497 ff; an unsigned note by Becker, Storms Papers.

[105] Strauch à Ramaeckers, 7. iv. 82, *ibid*.

replacement to take no steps to recognize Mirambo's authority.[106] The
Belgians let the matter rest, however, and no more trouble occurred; all
the expeditions that Mirambo later sent to the Karema region left the Belgians in peace.[107]

In July, 1882, Mirambo lost his long-time English advisor, Southon, who
was accidentally shot and died through lack of proper medical care, in
spite of the efforts of an English missionary and a German naturalist to
save him.[108] Although Southon had converted no Africans to his brand
of Christianity, the L.M.S. could take pride in his work in Africa. He
had done his best to make Mirambo live in peace, and if he had had more
support from the British in Zanzibar after the Carter affair, he might
have achieved notable results.

After Southon's death, the French Roman Catholic missionaries in East
Africa in March, 1884, followed up earlier tentative discussions by opening a mission station in Mirambo's territory near Urambo.[109] But by now
the African leader's life was drawing to a close and the mission was not
to play a significant role in the region.

IV

In 1883 Mirambo entered into a long and often interrupted struggle
that was to continue until his death. His Ngoni allies had been causing
him trouble since at least 1882.[110] He avoided a definite break with them
since they were useful against the Arabs, but after the defeat of Simba
they stole some of the booty and war began.[111] They were defeated at
first in campaigns that took Mirambo to the shores of Victoria, but the
victory was not to last: a new opponent who rose against Mirambo,
Kapera of Uyogo, called them to his aid.[112]

Illness prevented Mirambo from playing his usual role against this new
enemy. His brother, Kirunga, who led the army, lacked Mirambo's military talents and, in spite of his illness, the latter remained as active as

[106] Strauch à Storms, 23. v. 82 and 26. v. 82, *ibid.*
[107] For example, Storms à A.I.A., 16. iv. 84, *ibid.*
[108] Copplestone to L.M.S., 4 .viii. 82, L.M.S. Archives; Böhm, *Tanganjika*, 104.
[109] J. Cussac, *L'Apôtre de l'Ouganda. Le Père Lourdel* (Paris, 1944), 127–28.
[110] See above, p. 23.
[111] Hannington to C.M.S., 13. xi. 82, G3. A6/0 1, C.M.S. Archives; *Les Missions
Catholiques,* XV (1883), 200.
[112] Stokes to Stock, received 20. i. 85, G3. A6/0 2, I.M.S. Archives; A. Mackay,
"Log of a Voyage on the Nyanza," entries of 31. vii. 83 and 4. viii. 83, G3. A6/0 1,
ibid.; Shaw to L.M.S., 7. vii. 83, L.M.S. Archives.

possible until the end. One episode reported described an effort at peace after a hard fight before Kapera's stockade: Mirambo and a group of Masai who had been called in to replace the Ngoni as allies, approached the fort to negotiate and found themselves caught in ambush. But the shrewd Nyamwezi chief had foreseen the possibility and gave the signal to a waiting force he had prepared who drove the enemy away.[113]

Illness finally forced Mirambo to give up all part in this war. Realizing that his condition was serious, he called on the English and French missionaries for help, but his case was hopeless and he died on December 2, 1884, from an abscess of the throat.[114] Some claim that Mirambo died of poison, at the hand of either the Nyamwezi chief of Tabora, Siki,[115] or of the Arabs.[116] They must be ignored: Mirambo died of an illness known to the many Europeans who were with him before his death.

With the death of Mirambo, the territory formerly under his control soon freed itself from his successor's rule. His brother, Mpanda Sharo, or Kirunga, succeeded to power, but his was an inferior genius and he could not curb the rising strength of Kapera.[117] While Mpanda Sharo remained on good terms with Europeans, it was not enough to keep his realm together.[118] He ruled until 1890 when he was killed fighting the Ngoni. A German expedition, led by Emin Pasha, which was in the area then sent aid to Urambo, with the result that Urambo passed formally under German rule, with a son of Mirambo as the new chief.[119] This boy, only ten or eleven years old at the time, did not make an able ruler, and the Germans later had him removed and assumed effective control of the area themselves.[120]

In summing up his place in the history of East Africa, Mirambo can be best described as a remarkable individual who rose to power and dominance through his own talents and ability. He had to face continuing friction with the Arabs of East Africa, and deal with the new phenome-

[113] Cussac, *Lourdel,* 128 ff.

[114] *Ibid.,* 135; Stockes to Lang, 18. xiii. 84, G3. A6/0 2. C.M.S. Archives; François Coulbois, *Dix Années au Tanganyka* (Limoges, 1901), 51.

[115] G. Richelmann, "Die erst Durchquerung Äquatorial-Africas von West nach Ost," *Hermann von Wissmann* (A. Becker *et. al.,* Berlin, 1913), 54.

[116] Carnochan and Adamson, *Out of Africa,* 126.

[117] Capitaine Joubert, "De Kibanga à Bagomoyo," *Le Mouvement Antiesclavagiste,* (1888–89), 174; Stokes to Lang, 18. xii. 84, G3. A6/0 2, C.M.S. Archives.

[118] Shaw to L.M.S., 9. iii. 85, L.M.S. Archives; Cussac, *Lourdel,* 140.

[119] Wilhelm Langheld, *Zwanzig Jahre in deutschen Kolonien* (Berlin, 1909), 55 ff; Karl Hespers, *P. Schynse's letzte Reisen-Briefe und Tagenbuchblätter* (Köln, 1892), 8–9; Shaw to L.M.S., 10. vii. 90, L.M.S. Archives; Draper to L.M.S., 7. vii. 90, *Ibid.*

[120] Shaw to L.M.S., 27. iv. 95, *ibid.*

non of the European penetration of his country. He met both challenges well; the Arabs were never able to challenge him seriously; the Europeans generally respected him and wished to work with him. If it had not been for the death of Carter and Cadenhead, he might have played even a larger role with Europeans backing his authority. That his dominions crumbled with his death was no fault of his own; he built them following the customs of his area, adapting new conditions to increase his strength, and the fact that he won them at all, and peacefully administered them during much of his reign in the face of the existing conditions was an achievement that cannot be overlooked.

His epitaph by the missionary-trader, Stokes, who knew him well, is fitting:

> Mirambo was a most wonderful man. I know not his equal throughout the country. A wise ruler, a grand general for native warfare, every inch a soldier. Since Dr. Southon first went to live with him, from the wild lawless chief, he turned into the wise ruler, the careful general, the white man's true friend.[121]

[121] Stokes to Lang, 18. xii. 84, G3. A6/0 2, C.M.S. Archives.

Americans in Zanzibar: 1865–1915

During the American Civil War the American traders in Zanzibar lost the commanding position in the commerce of the island that they had maintained for many years.[1] Shortages of trading goods and high costs in the United States, plus the presence of Confederate raiders on the routes to East Africa, placed the Americans there in a difficult position. They had struggled to keep business alive, often importing their goods in British ships, but, although their credit remained sound, trade had seriously declined.

I

The recession of American interests did not last long, however. By 1867 their trade was recovering, in spite of heavy competition from Indian, British, German, French and other firms, and the American Consul, E. D. Ropes, thought the trade of the United States would soon regain its former magnitude.[2]

The French representative in Zanzibar, writing independently, corroborated this picture of returning American prosperity.[3] And in a speech in 1869, a leading citizen in the town of Salem gave confirming evidence: this Massachusetts center, he claimed, received a large percentage of the

[1] For the account of Americans in Zanzibar before 1865, see the present writer's studies in the Essex Institute *Historical Collections*, XCV (1959), 239–62, and XCVII (1961), 31–56, or in *Tanganyika Notes and Records*, 56 (1961), 93–108, and 57 (1961), 121–38.

[2] Ropes to State Department, 15. viii. 67, Foreign Affairs Section, National Archives, Washington, D. C. [hereafter SDA]. Ropes gives statistics, but as John Kirk said: "It is impossible to obtain accurate and reliable statistics of the trade of Zanzibar, everyone being interested in representing the imports and exports as less than they actually are." From R. Coupland, *The Exploitation of East Africa, 1856–1890* (London, 1939), 77. The statistics from American, British and French sources differ; therefore, as a rule, only the relative position of American trade, taken on the average, will be given here.

[3] Jablonski à M.A.E., 31. xii. 67, Correspondance Commercial, Zanzibar, t. 2, Archives, Ministère des Affaires Étrangères, Paris [hereafter M.A.E.].

ivory, gums, and hides coming into the United States — all products
sought after by Salem men in East Africa.[4]

The American traders were able to recover quickly because of the su-
periority of their main import into Zanzibar, cotton cloth. It remained,
in the words of the future Lord Lugard: "the very best cloth in the market and almost as strong as canvas." [5] German and Indian merchants had
made strong efforts to substitute their own cloth while American goods
were in short supply, but the local populations considered them of inferior quality and bought them only when there was no alternative.[6] Apart
from their cotton goods, the American traders had no other staples to keep
trade flowing after the Civil War and found it necessary to import specie
to buy the exports they desired.[7]

In diplomacy, the American representatives had little to do before the
early 1870's. The Consuls, who were almost always resident merchants,
were most interested in the renewed efforts of the British to further re-
strict the slave trading carried on from Zanzibar. A treaty of 1845 between Britain and Zanzibar prohibited the export of slaves from the Sultan's African dominions, but it did allow shipments to Zanzibar and
Pemba. Such a treaty was of course difficult to enforce, and the success
of the efforts of the Royal Navy in preventing the slave trade varied with
the numbers and activities of their ships in African waters.

In 1868, the navy, and the British Consul, Churchill, appeared to the
Americans to be determined to strike a hard blow against the illegal slave
trade — and perhaps even to attempt to abolish slavery itself. Of this,
all Americans in Zanzibar took the same view: such measures had to be
carried out gradually or Zanzibar would be thrown in chaos which would
threaten the continuance of American trade. In fact, in 1868, F. R. Webb,
the American representative, asked the State Department to send a vessel
to Zanzibar to protect American interests from any consequences of harsh
British policy. At the same time, he put in a good word for the slave
owners of Zanzibar: "The Arab property in Zanzibar consists largely in
slaves who work on the clove and cocoa nut plantations, are kindly treated,
and who with their owner and his children form a happy family." [8] The

---

[4] Robert S. Rantoul, "The Port of Salem," Essex Institute *Historical Collections*,
X (1869), 72.
[5] Margery Perham (ed.), *The Diaries of Lord Lugard* (London, 1959), I, 290.
[6] Jablonski à M.A.E., 20. ii. 64, Corr. Comm. Zanz., t. 2.
[7] Ropes to S.D., 15. viii. 67, SDA.
[8] Webb to S.D., 20. viii. 68, Ropes Papers, Peabody Museum, Salem, Mass. [here-
after P.M.].

Arabs did, of course, treat their slaves kindly; this was not the problem. What the British sought to mitigate was the devastation of the African interior caused by the gathering of slaves for Zanzibar and elsewhere. The State Department, realizing this, wrote a strong reply to Webb's dispatch:

> If it be true as you suppose that the British Government is sedulously engaged in endeavoring to induce the Sultan to abolish slavery in the Island of Zanzibar, neither this country nor any other can have any reason to complain of the proceeding. So far from protesting against it, the influence of this government would be exerted in its favor.[9]

The British did not actually try to abolish slavery in Zanzibar, but when they moved against the slave trade they found, in spite of the official view of the United States, that the American residents were not disposed to cooperate with them.

The American attitude to British efforts against the slave trade appears unusual, especially so soon after the Civil War, particularly since many of the Americans in Zanzibar had served in the armed forces of the North. Their position becomes understandable when the British methods to combat the slave trade in East African waters are understood. Admittedly, the Royal Navy with the few ships at its disposal had a difficult task in tracking down slavers in the western Indian Ocean. The real problem, however, came when an Arab vessel was boarded and an investigation of its business carried out. All Arab vessels had slaves in their crews (this was legal), and thus very careful proceedings were required for all but the most obvious slaving ships. Before 1870, the investigations were highly unsatisfactory and injustice often resulted. The first difficulty was that of language; native interpreters were necessary, and in this period there were serious doubts of their honesty since prize money was given to the officers and men for every slave ship convicted and condemned. The legal process, in theory, had to be carried out in a prize court, but until the late 1860's the nearest courts for the East African patrol were in Aden and Cape Town. Distance made conveyance there impracticable and so, if judged unseaworthy, an Arab dhow could be destroyed on the spot. Of course, by British standards all Arab dhows were unseaworthy. Even if the vessel was brought to court, conviction was almost automatic since the Arabs did not understand the British system and received little help. To this unfortunate situation was added an

---

[9] Seward to Webb, 12. xi. 68, SDA.

occurrence frequently mentioned in the literature of the time: the looting
of helpless Arab dhows by British crews, whether they were guilty of carrying slaves or not.[10]

Thus, in 1868 and 1869, whether from the English hatred of the slave
trade or their excess zeal to gain prize money, Arab trading vessels oper-
ating from Zanzibar suffered greatly. F. R. Webb estimated that seventy
ships had been burned in one year, many of them innocent, and he complained that ravages such as these would soon ruin all the trade of Zanzibar.[11] Fortunately for the Americans and other traders, the British at
last took steps to end them, stirred, perhaps, by a Foreign Office official's
comments:

> In my opinion the system on which our naval officers are now acting in carry-
> ing out the Slave Trade suppression duty on the East Coast of Africa, is one
> which cannot be justified, and which would not be tolerated for a month by
> any European power if their vessels were seized and condemned without a
> hearing in the manner in which Zanzibar and other native Dhows have for
> the last few years been treated by our cruisers.[12]

Accordingly, orders were sent that trials were necessary unless in very
exceptional circumstances, and a Vice-Admiralty Court was set up in
Zanzibar.[13]

John Kirk, the British representative in Zanzibar, carried out these orders, and innocent dhows were set free. The Americans then quieted
down, but they were again disillusioned when the British, a few years
later, introduced new measures against the slave trade. A British histo-
rian once said of Britain and the slave trade: "That her motives were disinterested can scarcely be questioned," [14] but, seeing the conduct of
British crews in East African waters, the Americans understandably enter-
tained a skeptical opinion of the disinterested motives of the British.
Kirk, who seldom got along well with Americans, increased their mistrust;
at the end of 1870 he wrote the Foreign Office that all the other consuls
were upset at his success with the Sultan who now "treated this Agency
with proper respect and as taking precedence in everything without

---

[10] See W. Cope Devereux, *A Cruise in the "Gorgon"* (London, 1869), especially
128–29, 268; Captain Colomb, *Slave Catching in the Indian Ocean* (London, 1873),
passim.

[11] Webb to Seward, 10. iii. 69, SDA; Webb to Ropes, 13. iv. 69, Ropes Papers.

[12] Note of W. Wylde, 1. vii. 69, F.O. 84/1307, Public Record Office, London.

[13] F.O. to Kirk, 25. ii. 70, F.O. 84/1325.

[14] William L. Mathieson, *Great Britain and the Slave Trade, 1839–1865* (London,
1929), 1.

question."[15]   The Americans must have found this attitude increasingly hard to live with.

II

This unfortunate legacy became prominent in 1873 when the British government decided to take firm action to end the sea-borne slave trade in East African waters. In the previous year, when preparing plans, the British asked the American government and other powers for their coop-eration in ending the slave trade. The British also thought that legitimate trade in this region would hurt the slave trade, and requested the United States and other interested governments to aid in establishing a line of steamers to East African ports.[16]

The Secretary of State, Hamilton Fish, was receptive to the British schemes, at least with regard to the slave trade. He told the British am-bassador he would instruct the American representative in Zanzibar to give support in the ending of the sea-borne slave trade and would send an American warship to Zanzibar to help. However, he declined to act on the proposed steamship line: he said the United States supported pri-vate enterprise in such matters and that Congress would not change our traditional policy for distant East Africa.[17]   The orders to the Americans concerned accorded with the Secretary's pledges: Commander Wilson of the U.S.S. *Yantic* soon headed for Zanzibar to aid Webb in cooperating with the British emissary "in every proper manner which may tend to-wards the success of his mission."[18]

The *Yantic* was already there when the British mission, headed by Sir Bartle Frere, reached Zanzibar in January, 1873. Wilson had taken ad-vantage of his early arrival to try to act "Stanley and Livingstone over again" — by signing the desired treaty before Frere arrived. He failed, so Frere claimed, because of the machinations of the American Consul, J. F. Webb, whose interpreter when presenting the Sultan the "long and strong despatch" prepared by Wilson, robbed it of all its force. For the interpreter merely asked the Sultan to uphold the provisions of the 1845

---

[15] Coupland, *The Exploitation of East Africa*, 99.
[16] Granville to Thornton, 16. ii. 72, F.O. 84/1386. Sir John Gray, "Early Connec-tions Between the United States and East Africa," *Tanganyika Notes and Records*, 22 (1946), 80–83 and Coupland, *The Exploiting of East Africa*, 182 ff, deal with this episode.
[17] Thornton to Granville, 30. iii. 72, enclosing Fish to Thornton, 29. iii. 72, F.O. 84/1355.
[18] Fish to Webb, 26. x. 72, and 2. iv. 72, SDA.

treaty, the treaty the British were out to change. The Sultan, of course, agreed, and Wilson considered his work in Zanzibar accomplished.

In due time Webb reported to the State Department that he had carried out his instructions.[19] His actions seem strange, even for an American trader who resented British influence in Zanzibar. Apparently his great dislike of it motivated his failure to carry out instructions. In a private letter he gave his opinion of the affair:

> I have this d----d slave business on my hands. I hate this job . . . I think our Government is made a cat's paw of in this matter — to rake out the chestnuts from the fire.

He went on to say that he accompanied Wilson's group to the Sultan, but in the course of the talks he once became so angry that he walked out.[20] The crux of the affair was that America's representative was a private trader who expected to use his position only as a means of aiding commerce. When he was instructed to act in a political matter in a way which he felt might hurt American trading interests, he would not carry out orders, particularly if a dutiful following of them would aid the British who, in his opinion, were already too powerful in Zanzibar.

Webb therefore persisted in resisting when Frere arrived. He "declined all cooperation" and even refused to return the courtesy calls of members of the mission. Moreover, he told the British that his instructions allowed him to do no more than he had already done in presenting Wilson's note to the Sultan. Wilson remined in Zanzibar for a time, but was of little use to Frere; he described him as a friend, but "not a very efficient ally, for though a shrewd man his habits and manners did not give much weight to his advice." In less diplomatic language, one of Frere's aides said of Wilson that he had orders "to cooperate cordially, and carries them out literally by visiting H. Majesty's ships and Consul impartially and getting drunk invariably." [21]

Frere soon discovered that Webb was not alone in his opposition; he wrote:

[19] Frere to Granville, 1. ii. 73, F.O. 84/1389; Wilson to the Secretary of War, 16. xii. 72, Naval Records Collection, Box 3, Navy Department Section, National Archives, Washington D. C. [hereafter NDA]; Webb to S.D., 17. xii. 72, SDA.

[20] Webb to Ropes, 18. xii. 72, Ropes Papers.

[21] Frere to Granville, 1. ii. 73, 10. ii. 73, enclosing Wilson to Frere, 20. i. 73, Wilson to Sultan of Zanzibar, 11. xii. 72, report of Pelly and Kirk, 20. i. 73, F.O. 84/1389; Euan Smith to Mackinnon, 17. i. 73, Mackinnon Papers, School of Oriental and African Studies, University of London.

one of the best and most respectable foreign merchants [said his compatriots had] . . . entire hostility to our efforts for repressing it [the slave trade] — not that they approve of it in the abstract . . . They wish it left alone, not from wishing to participate in it or its profits, but because when the slave trade is flourishing other trade flourishes, when the slave trade is depressed or persecuted other trade is dull.[22]

This merchant's nationality was not mentioned, but his line of reasoning was that pursued by all the American traders in Zanzibar.

When these events were reported to the Foreign Office, immediate inquiries were made in Washington about the activities of their consul. But when questioned about Webb's course of action, Fish could say only that Webb had written he was carrying out his instructions.[23] This did not suffice for Lord Granville and he ordered his ambassador to express his dissatisfaction, at the same time acknowledging and praising Wilson's efforts.[24] But recriminations apparently went too far, for Fish began to uphold Webb in the face of foreign critics; he brought up the fact, as he had earlier, that the British had given him only general information of Frere's plans, and not a full report of his instructions, with the result that American support could not be specific. Fish concluded: "So far as I am aware, Mr. Webb has fully and faithfully complied with the instructions [sent]." This strong reply caused the British ambassador to retract his complaints about American cooperation; he said he did not mean to infer Webb had deliberately misinterpreted Wilson's note and that the native interpreter was probably the guilty party.[25]

When the American ambassador in London followed this matter up by restating Fish's views, and again referred to American ignorance of Frere's instructions, the British retracted. They told him they had wished merely to report Webb's actions and not to indulge in unnecessary recrimination and informed him, in part, of Frere's instructions. The British ambassador in Washington was soon ordered to impart to Fish full details of the mission to Zanzibar,[26] a wise move on the part of the Foreign Office since

[22] Frere to Granville, 7. v. 73, F.O. 84/1391.

[23] Thornton to Granville, 3. iii. 73, F.O. 84/1392.

[24] Granville to Thornton, 17. iii. 73 and Thornton to Granville, 7. iv. 73, enclosing Thornton to Fish, 5. iv. 73, *ibid.*

[25] Thornton to Granville, 14. iv. 73, enclosing Fish to Thornton, 8. iv. 73 and Thornton to Fish, 10. iv. 73, and Thornton to Granville, 15. iv. 73, enclosing Fish to Thornton, 14. iv. 73, *ibid.*

[26] Granville to Thornton, 29. iv. 73, and 2. v. 73, F.O. 84/1392 and F. O. 84/1393 respectively.

Fish was suspicious of Frere's mission and thought that the British had
motives other than the suppression of the slave trade.[27] The British, in
the end, dropped the whole thing and adopted the policy of working for
American support in the future conduct of Frere's mission.[28]

Soon after, J. F. Webb became ill and had to leave Zanzibar "nearly at
the point of death." [29] His successor as American representative, F. R.
Webb, an experienced Zanzibar trader and a naval veteran of the Civil
War,[30] took an entirely different view of the Frere mission. He had
gained a position of great influence with the Sultan during his years in
Zanzibar and was willing to aid the British as much as possible. John
Kirk, carrying on the negotiations after the departure of Frere, welcomed
his support and worked closely with him. In a series of interviews, Webb
urged the Sultan to give in to the British demands; admitting that he
felt them rather strong, he wisely pointed out that resistance was futile.
The Sultan delayed and in the end was sent an ultimatum by the British.
Webb again advised immediate compliance and the Sultan finally accepted terms. John Kirk praised Webb's role in the settlement — "to
which, in great measure, I ascribe the favourable termination of these
negotiations." This was an exaggeration since he could have won out
without American support, but there was no doubt that Webb had has-
tened the Sultan's surrender. Kirk also saw the American trader's real
motive: the second Webb was wiser than the first, for he realized the British were determined to act and came to the conclusion that in the interests of trade, it was best to have the matter settled quickly.[31] Thus an
unpleasant incident precipitated by the unprofessional American diplomatic service, was closed and the United States, so recently at war over
slavery at home, was saved from appearing before the world as opposed
to the abolition of the slave trade in East Africa.

In the 1870's the American traders in Zanzibar continued the struggle
for a larger share of the trade of the island. A new event, however, in-
tervened to make their task harder: the Suez Canal. Opened in 1869, it
revolutionized trade in East Africa; regular steamship service now con-
nected Zanzibar with Europe and European trading vessels could reach
East Africa in much less time than the American. As F. R. Webb com-

[27] Thornton to Granville, 5. v. 73, F.O. 84/1369.
[28] Granville to Thornton, 9. vii. 73, *ibid.*
[29] F.R. Webb to S.D., 8. iv. 73, SDA.
[30] For a biographical note on Webb, George B. Putnam, "Salem Vessels and their
Voyages," Essex Institute *Historical Collections,* LX (1924), 22.
[31] Kirk to F.O., 27. v. 73, 1. vi. 73, 5. vi. 73, F.O. 84/1374; Webb to S.D., 16. iv.
73, Kirk, to Webb, 5. vi. 73, SDA.

plained, it "raised the old scratch with our markets . . . [since] every little Hindoo now puts his oar in . . ." Indian merchants no longer had to dispose of their merchandise through foreign agents; they could deal directly with visiting steamers. The risks were small and profits good, so that American interests were bound to suffer.[32]

In the year 1870, an era came to a close: the last vessel from Salem, the *Glide,* left Zanzibar and arrived in Salem harbor in May.[33] After that date the Salem firms still operated in Zanzibar, but their sailing vessels were based in other American ports. Transportation by sail continued in use in this time of steam, since ships under canvas could carry bulk goods, such as hides, very cheaply, but other items purchased by American firms were increasingly brought to the United States in foreign vessels.[34] The present writer has found no record of any American steam vessel trading in Zanzibar during the nineteenth century.

But the new conditions created by the Suez Canal were met and overcome by the Americans in Zanzibar. In the early 1870's they secured for themselves most of the gum copal and ivory in the Zanzibar market.[35] In his report for the year ending in September, 1871, the American Consul stated that the losses caused by the Civil War were nearly recovered and the only matter to worry American traders was the rising price of their cotton goods.[36] As mentioned in the present writer's earlier studies, the Americans in East Africa traded not only with Zanzibar, but had agents in other parts of the coast. At this time, in fact, they were profiting very considerably from their trading establishments on the island of Madagascar, where American cottons were the one essential import and where foreign merchants, to meet American competition, had to sell American cloth.[37]

American progress was not continuous, however. In April, 1872, the worst hurricane in the history of Zanzibar struck the island.[38] The many

[32] Webb to Ropes, 6. x. 70, Ropes Papers.

[33] Chas. S. Osgood, and H. M. Batchelder, *Historical Sketch of Salem* (Salem, 1879), 167.

[34] A letter of T. Stevens, 24. ii. 89, in the *New York World,* 14. iv. 89. For the decline of Salem as a port, Robert G. Albion, "From Sails to Spindles: Essex County in Transition," Essex Institute *Historical Collections,* XCV (1959), 115–36.

[35] J. F. Webb to Ropes, 29. v. 71 and 20. vi. 71, Ropes Papers. Webb provides here a good illustration of the American merchant mind: his comment on a busy social season in Zanzibar — that there was no point in "calling upon people out of whom there is not a dollar to be made."

[36] Report of the Commerce of Zanzibar for the Year Ending 30. ix. 71, SDA.

[37] A. Grandidier, "Le Commerce de Madagascar," *Bulletin de la Société de Géographie,* 6e–III (1872), 210–11.

[38] For details, Coupland, *The Exploitation of East Africa,* 56–7.

local residents in debt to American traders or delivering them materials on contract, could not meet their obligations and the three local American firms were badly shaken. One, indeed, never recovered and went into bankruptcy.[39] After the storm, Kirk reported that the two remaining firms owed $200,000 and $400,000, respectively, to creditors in Zanzibar.[40] This state of affairs brought a rueful comment from one of the American merchants:

> The good old times, when we could run up a $300,000 debt and think of it only once in six months when we gave a new note have ended, and we have got to have the hard money right on the spot.[41]

These setbacks, however, did not long hinder them. Even though their cottons did become very expensive in 1873, they continued to control the ivory market in Zanzibar, and thus remained vitally important in the island's economic life. A main reason for their resiliency was their close working relationship with some of the leading local Indian merchants. (Sir Bartle Frere had remarked that the Indian "sometimes stands to the foreign firm in a relation more like that of a partner than a mere broker, agent or go-between." [42]) The well-known Taria Topan,[43] probably the most important Indian merchant of Zanzibar, was described by Kirk as "American in all his interests." [44] But Topan bothered them because he controlled the market for their goods. The Americans, however, played the Indians off against one another whenever possible and managed to keep their independence.[45] That the friction was only a minor matter in the 1870's is clear from an American trader's urging Topan to hurry back from a visit to India since no other merchant of Zanzibar knew and treated American interests so well.[46]

Working in this manner, American business improved in the late 1870's. Then came another new thing: the growing demand for American kero-

---

[39] Gertrude Ward, *Letters of Bishop Tozer* (London, 1902), 271; Guillois à M.A.E., 25. v. 74, Corr. Comm., Zanz., t. 3.

[40] Kirk to F.O., 22. v. 72, F.O. 84/1357.

[41] J. F. Webb to Ropes, 19. v. 72, Ropes Papers. For the "good old times" referred to, see Bennett, "Americans in Zanzibar, 1845–1865," Essex Institute *Historical Collections*, XCVIII (1961), 46.

[42] Frere to Granville, 7. v. 73, F.O. 84/1391.

[43] See L. W. Hollingsworth, *The Asians of East Africa* (London, 1960), 140.

[44] Kirk to Mackinnon, 25. v. 79, Mackinnon Papers.

[45] Hathorne to Arnold, Hines and Co., 1. vi. 77 and Hathorne to Emmerton, 29. vi. 77, Hathorne Papers, P.M.

[46] Hathorne to Topan, 27. vii. 77, *ibid.*

sene for lighting purposes in East Africa. A trade report of the mid-1860's listed imports of kerosene valued at only $500; [47] by 1872 imports amounted to 2000 cases a year; by 1878, to 25,000, with demand well in excess of the supply. A three-cent tin lamp was sold for use with the kerosene. Since one cent's worth of kerosene would last two nights, the demand for vegetable oils till now customary for lighting quickly fell away in Zanzibar and on parts of the coast.[48] The trade in American cottons now also revived. In the interior new markets were opened and many a traveller commented on the spread of American cloth, among them Joseph Thomson, who observed that American cottons were "fast hustling England out of the African market." Keith Johnston, commenting in the same vein, blamed this state of affairs on the "thin, and comparatively poor and worthless Manchester cotton." [49] By the late 1870's American traders imported, on the average, goods worth about $500,000 and exported goods worth between $500,000 and $1,000,000 and American shipping to handle the merchandise from Zanzibar included from twenty-five to forty vessels a year.[50]

III

Conditions remained much the same in the years leading up to 1885 and the European scramble for East Africa. Three American firms, Arnold, Hines and Co. of New York, George Ropes and Co. of Boston, and Ropes, Emmerton and Co. of Salem, had regular agents for trade in Zanzibar. The oldest foreign firm in Zanzibar, that of John Bertram of Salem, whose interests in Zanzibar dated from the 1830's, closed in 1882 when he died.[51] Ropes, Emmerton and Co. was organized to carry on his work and thus the Salem interests in Zanzibar did not suffer from the loss of Bertram. The Americans remained important in trade, but were now

[47] Ropes to S.D., 15. viii. 67, SDA.

[48] Hathorne to Ryder, 19. ix. 77, Hathorne Papers.

[49] Hathorne to Bertram, 16. x. 78, *ibid.*; Joseph Thomson, *To the Central African Lakes and Back* (London, 1881), I, 36; Keith Johnston, "Notes of a Trip from Zanzibar to Usambura . . . ," *Proceedings of the Royal Geographical Society*, I (1879), 545.

[50] Hathorne to S.D., 30. ix. 79, SDA; Thomson to Shufeldt, 24. x. 79, in "Cruise of the Ticonderoga," II, NDA; Charles Courret, *A l'Est et à l'Ouest dans l'Océan Indien* (Paris, 1884), 128–29. Some of the vessels listed called at Zanzibar several times in one year; the figure given here lists each caller as a separate vessel, even though it had been there before.

[51] See the comments on his life in Essex Institute *Historical Collections*, XXI (1884), 81–96.

lost to view in the large numbers of Europeans coming to Zanzibar: in 1883, a list of Europeans on the island mentioned forty-seven Englishmen, seventeen French, eleven Germans, and only four Americans.[52]

In the early 1880's the main competition for the American share of trade came from German merchants, whose firms in Zanzibar grew from two to five between 1881 and 1885.[53] They tried, but in vain, to woo Taria Topan away from his American friends.[54] Topan, however, began now to cause the American firms a great deal of trouble by playing one against the other as they competed for his services, and exploiting the situation to make additional profit.[55] So commanding was his position in Zanzibar that he was able to run all trading to his own benefit, controlling, for one thing, all sales of kerosene to local retailers, and, for another, bringing in supplies of cheap Indian cotton to dislodge the more expensive American goods from the market.[56] In the opinion of one Belgian observer, such efforts had been so successful that American cotton had been almost entirely replaced,[57] but in the ivory market the American firms continued to dominate, having orders for 12,000 pounds of ivory a month and normally filling them without difficulty.[58] The value of American exports and imports remained much the same as it had been in the late 1870's.[59]

The American representatives in their diplomatic functions were not called upon to deal with problems of any gravity from 1873 to 1885. Some difficulty, however, arose over that controversial naturalized American, Henry Morton Stanley. On his first trip into East Africa, he had had few dealings with the American officials of the island, but he left in Zanzibar a considerable legacy of dislike because of his quarrels with John Kirk.[60] Thus, when he returned to East Africa to start his great trip across the continent (1874–1877), he met with no friendly reception on the part of Kirk or indeed of most of the British. Once in the interior, he engaged, for perhaps insufficient reasons, in some particularly bloody battles with Africans and since he travelled under both the American and

[52] E. D. Ropes, Jr. to his parents, 20. viii. 83, Ropes Papers.
[53] Ledoulx à M.A.E., 17. i. 85, Politique, Zanzibar, t. 7, M.A.E.
[54] Ropes, Jr. to parents, 28. ix. 84, Rope Papers.
[55] Ropes, Jr. to parents, 23. iii. 84, *Ibid.*
[56] Ropes, Jr. to parents, 27. x. 84, 15. xi. 84, 23. xi. 84; Ropes, Jr. to Ropes, 25. v. 83; Bachelder to Ropes, 17. ii. 82: all in Ropes Papers.
[57] "Notes," Storms Papers, Musée Royal de l'Afrique Centrale, Tervuren, Belgium.
[58] William H. Beehler, *The Cruise of the Brooklyn* (Philadelphia, 1885), 172.
[59] Bachelder to S.D., 9. ix. 81; Cheney's Trade Report for the Year Ending 30. vi. 84; Cheney to S.D., 18. xi. 84: all in SDA.
[60] See Sir Reginald Coupland, *Livingstone's Last Journey* (London, 1947), 147 .

British flags, popular pressure in Britain brought it about that Kirk was instructed to deliver the following message to the American consul:

> I have the honour to inform you that in consequence of the painful impression produced in England by Mr. Stanley's recent proceedings in the interior of Africa and of his collisions with native tribes as reported in his letters I have been directed by the Earl of Derby to endeavor to convey to Mr. Stanley if any opportunity of communication should open an intimation that he has no authority to make use of the British flag as giving countenance to his proceedings.

There was, of course, no way to reach Stanley, and, though Hathorne, the American Consul, promised to do all he could in forwarding this message,[61] there is no evidence that Stanley ever received it.

Stanley returned to Zanzibar after he had succeeded in reaching the mouth of the Congo. He became a good friend of Hathorne's and the latter has some interesting remarks to make about the reception of the American explorer by Kirk. The British Consul could not control his dislike for Stanley and the British subjects in Zanzibar usually followed his lead, although officers of the Royal Navy in Zanzibar did give the explorer a reception. As Hathorne said: "the air here is so thoroughly impregnated with '*Kirkism*' that his stay here has not been very 'gay and festive.'" Hathorne had reasons of his own to dislike Kirk, over and above the shabby treatment of Stanley, for Kirk looked down with contempt upon the merchant-consuls of the United States and went out of his way to affront them, as Hathorne proved in recording a humorous incident. The American merchants used the roofs of their business houses to dry hides for shipping home to the United States and Hathorne wrote:

> then Kirk can't bear the "American stinking hides." His aristocratic nose we often see go in the air as he goes under our windows making some such a remark to whoever may be with him.[62]

[61] Kirk to Hathorne, 11. xii. 76 and Hathorne to Kirk, 13. xii. 76, N–23, Zanzibar Archives. See also, Gray, "Early Connections Between the United States and East Africa," 78–9.

[62] Hathorne to Emmerton, 12. xii. 77 and Hathorne to Ropes, 6. ii. 79, Hathorne Papers. Hathorne kept in touch with Stanley when the latter was working for Leopold in the Congo. He made this interesting report: "The very night after you sailed the Sultan went to K[irk].'s house with only a single lantern, and a soldier following, he spent one and one-half hours there and our mutual friend T. T[opan] told me the next day that he was *sure* K. knew all the Sultan did about your movements." See Hathorne to Stanley, 29. v. 79, Hathorne Papers. Hathorne made sure no one

The incident is insignificant, of course, but it does explain the continual retaliatory sniping at him by American residents.

In 1876, the State Department made a change in its management of the Consulate at Zanzibar that upset all the local American residents. For the first time in many years a non-trader was made Consul, William Riley of Virginia, and Kirk reported "the American traders here look with undisguised annoyance on the arrival among them of an independent official." Kirk also wondered, in view of the limited American interests in Zanzibar, just why such an official had been sent.[63] When the British ambassador followed this question up in Washington, he found the answer in a chain of events characteristic of the American diplomatic system. For it was, in reality, no sign of renewed official interest in Zanzibar; Riley had been appointed to another post, but when the Senate failed to confirm the nomination, he was given the Zanzibar office which was vacant at that time. In Zanzibar, he fared as had non-trading officials before him. He soon tired of his poorly paid and remote post and returned to the United States.[64] His replacement was a trader.

The slavery question, long dormant, arose again in 1878 to complicate Anglo-American relations in Zanzibar. At that time the merchants of the island, European and American, had a hard time to find laborers for their business operations. The many caravans leaving for the interior of Africa had brought about an acute labor shortage and caused the cost of hire to rise one hundred per cent in a year and one-half. The merchants affected then presented a petition to the Sultan, admitting they could make no complaint if free men wished to work in caravans, but that they did feel the Sultan could prevent the slaves of Zanzibar from doing so. Most of the laborers used by the merchants were slaves paid by their owners who arranged the terms of hire and they were the only hands available in Zanzibar. With the increase in caravans for the interior, they began to look for employment in them on their own and often left without consulting their masters. Thus the merchants in their petition suggested the following: an official was to check all hiring, to see if individuals were free to sign on; all caravans were to leave Zanzibar at a single designated point so that they might be checked again; and,

intercepted his messages to Stanley; he sent him a letter dated 28. vi. 79 inside of three envelopes addressed to another person.

[63] Kirk to Derby, 4. v. 76, F.O. 84/1453.
[64] Lister to Kirk, 18. viii. 76, enclosing Thornton to Derby, 13. vii. 76, Q–15, Zanzibar Archives; Hathorne to Kirk, 8. v. 76, N–23, *ibid.*

finally, all caravans were to give twenty-four hours' notice of their departure.[65]

The petition seems innocent enough; it aimed only at regulating conditions in Zanzibar and called for no new measures to make slaves of free men. But Kirk, perhaps motivated by his antipathy toward Americans, called it "a hollow sham to cover a movement in favour of the Slave Trade" and a proposal of a "most arbitrary law for the protection of a few slave owners with whom the Memorialists have contracts for the employment of slave labor." "This memorial," added Kirk, "would be contemptible were it not for the fact that the names of two of my official colleagues . . . [were included]." Receptive to the petition at first, the Sultan in the end bowed to Kirk's advice, as was usual, and rejected it.[66]

When the Foreign Office received Kirk's reports, they immediately instructed their ambassador in Washington to lodge a complaint. The State Department had no information about the petition, but replied that it opposed the slave trade and would investigate.[67] After learning the details, the authorities in Washington sent Hathorne a strong reprimand for the part he had taken in "a movement having for its apparent object the retention of your fellow men in hopeless bondage." [68] But the State Department's grounds were not quite valid since most of the slaves who went inland and survived the rigors of their journeys returned later to Zanzibar; their masters took a share of their pay just as they did when the slaves worked on the island. The British had put the case in terms that could not be refused, however, and, as was usual, the Americans in Zanzibar got little support from Washington.[69]

A new quarrel over slavery occurred at the very end of 1878. An American whaler, the *Laconia*, dropping anchor in Zanzibar harbor for provisions, was boarded and searched by men from the Royal Navy who found two men from the Comoro Islands on board, whom they took to be slaves.

[65] Sparhawk, Hathorne, Goldsmith [plus foreign merchants] to Sultan of Zanzibar, 2. i. 78, Sultan's Correspondence, *ibid.* For Hathorne's explanations, Hathorne to Arnold, Hines and Co., 6. ii. 78, Hathorne Papers.

[66] Kirk to Derby, 9. i. 78, 1. ii. 78, enclosing Sultan of Zanzibar to Hathorne, 16. i. 78, F.O. 84/1514. Episodes like this motivated this statement by a later American resident of Zanzibar: "I hear that soon Zanzibar is to be honored by the presence again of His Honor, Sir John Kirk, who will occupy the position of Sultan of Zanzibar again about Sept. 1st." Quoted from Ropes, Jr. to parents, 30. vi. 83, Ropes Papers.

[67] Lister to Kirk, 8. vii. 78, enclosing Thornton to Salisbury, 10. vi. 78, Q–19, Zanzibar Archives.

[68] Seward to Hathorne, 26. viii. 78, SDA.

[69] See Bennett, "Americans in Zanzibar: 1845–1865," 43.

They removed them from the vessel. By right, of course, such a procedure required the permission of the American Consul in Zanzibar, but no effort was made to secure it. Hathorne at once sent a strong protest to Kirk, reiterating the statement of the captain of the *Laconia* that the men were not slaves as far as he was concerned. But Kirk, after studying the matter, was convinced that they were slaves and remarked pointedly that he was "aware that American officials and others in these parts are in the habit of buying slaves and that they maintain this is not forbidden by their law." However, he recognized that the British had no jurisdiction over the men from the Comoroes since they had not had the American Consul's leave to search, and accordingly he had them released.[70] Kirk may have been right about the two men, but he had no proof that "American officials and others" participated in the buying of slaves and never mentioned it in his dispatches.[71] It is true that American whalers were notorious in the nineteenth century for ill-treating their crews, and the Africans they employed, and often robbed them of their wages, but that had nothing to do with the slave trade and Kirk was wise to let the matter drop. When the State Department heard of the affair they fully upheld Hathorne's actions, while the Foreign Office, for its part, at once disavowed the right of the Navy to have acted in this instance.[72] No more such events are reported at Zanzibar.

The next year, 1879, was marked by the visit to Zanzibar, for the first time in many years, of an official American mission: Commodore Shufeldt of the U.S.S. *Ticonderoga* was sent on a round-Africa trip with instructions to visit places that had no American representation and territories that had long-standing treaties with the United States with the eventual aim of increasing American trade.[73] The State Department's knowledge of Zanzibar before the time of this trip was so limited as to be amusing. The officials there, for instance, noticed while preparing for Shufeldt's voyage that certain changes had occurred in the political structure of Zanzibar since the American-Zanzibar treaty of 1833 and raised the ques-

[70] Kirk to Salisbury, 28. xii. 78, F.O. 84/1515; Kirk to F.O., 2. i. 79, enclosing Hathorne to Kirk, 31. xii. 78, Statement of the Captain of the *Laconia*, 28. xii. 78, and Kirk to Hathorne, 2. ii. 79, Q–22, Zanzibar Archives.

[71] The United States occasionally sent a vessel to investigate rumors of American citizens participating in the slave trade; these expeditions never learned of any guilty Americans — and they always checked with the British Consul. For example, Ropes, Jr. to Holmwood, 26. ii. 87, E–98, Zanzibar Archives.

[72] Payson to Hathorne, 27. iii. 79 and 7. vii. 79, SDA.

[73] "Cruise of the Ticonderoga," I, Instructions.

tion: "What were the political events which led to the change of residence of the sovereign and when did they take place?" [74] The political events, the division of the realm of Zanzibar and Muscat into two, had occurred early in the 1860's, unnoticed, apparently, by the State Department! If they now learned of the changes, they did not show it. Shufeldt wrote from Zanzibar that "Zanzibar is in Africa, and not in Muscat as even the State Department seems to think." [75] Yet, two years later, the American Consul found it necessary to protest that the Department still addressed his letters to Zanzibar *in* Muscat, causing lengthy delay.[76]

Shufeldt arrived in Zanzibar in October and remained for fifteen days. Kirk estimated that his mission had no great success, although it could have done much to increase American trade and to raise its prestige, since "Commodore Shufeldt although seemingly a man of considerable common-sense is devoid of the tact and address needed for the occasion." [77] Shufeldt's reports give a different impression: the Sultan was cordial to him and they enjoyed satisfactory talks on the treaty of 1833 which was continued in its original form since the terms pleased both the Sultan and the American community in Zanzibar. Shufeldt did notice, however, the great decline in American influence on the island; as he put it: "The American flag is growing smaller and smaller." [78] An odd bit of information about the visit is supplied by the French representative in Zanzibar. He said Shufeldt told the Sultan that he could count on the United States for aid if Zanzibar's independence were ever threatened.[79] There seems to be little justification for this assertion, but, though Shufeldt might promise, the United States, as the Sultan was soon to learn, might not necessarily deliver.

The Americans now began to take fright at the political developments which followed the treaties Carl Peters made in what is present-day Tanganyika at the end of 1884. For these accords led to the establishment of a German protectorate administered by a German company in

[74] Evarts to Thompson, 9. xi. 78, Domestic Letters, SDA.
[75] "Journal No. 2," 10. x. 79, Shufeldt Papers, Library of Congress, Washington, D.C.
[76] Bechelder to S.D., 22. vii. 81, SDA.
[77] Kirk to F.O., 15. x. 79 and 23. x. 79, Q–22, Zanzibar Archives.
[78] "Journal No. 2," 21. x. 78; Shufeldt to Sec. of Navy, 25. x. 79 and 28. x. 79, in "Cruise of the Ticonderoga," II; Charles O. Paullin, *Diplomatic Negotiations of American Naval Officers, 1778–1883* (Baltimore, 1912), 354; Russell M. Smith, Robert Wilson Schufeldt and the Opening of Korea" (University of Virginia, M.A., 1953), 66–9.
[79] Ledoulx à M.A.E., 16. x. 80, Polit., Zanzibar, t. 5.

the area behind the coast opposite Zanzibar, which the Americans feared was a serious threat to their position. The Germans were not noted for their liberal views of trade, while the attitude of the Zanzibar government had always been satisfactory to the Americans. The Sultan knew it and strove energetically to gain some American support in those troubled times. To this end he wrote the Secretary of State to ask what the United States would do in view of the new situation in East Africa. The answer of Secretary Bayard gave him little comfort: merely that the United States would not agree to any changes imposed on Zanzibar against its wishes.[80] This meant the United States would take no steps to aid Zanzibar, where her interests were small: Washington lodged no protest when the German navy, with the sanction of the British, forced Zanzibar to agree to the new German protectorate.[81]

With the new political alignment in East Africa, the Germans, backed by the British, succeeded in modifying Zanzibar's trade treaties with foreign powers. The role of the British was that of protecting the interests of Zanzibar as much as possible,[82] and the two European powers then sought to have the United States bring their treaty of 1833 in line with the new agreements. They informed the State Department that the changes would improve conditions at Zanzibar for foreigners and would encourage the Sultan to take an active interest in building up trade. Britain and Germany urged quick action so that all would be ready for the coming fiscal year in Zanzibar. But the State Department was not impressed and turned down the joint request, for, as Bayard noted, the United States wanted no part in an arrangement whereby the two European powers were taking over a measure of control of Zanzibar's administration. This impasse did not last for very long, however. The Department realized that action was necessary, and instructed the American representative, F. M. Cheney, to bring the United States in line with the new situation. A new treaty was agreed upon in Zanzibar on July 3, 1886, and ratified in 1888, that gave the United States the rights of the most favored nation.[83]

[80] Kirk to Salisbury, 21. viii. 85, enclosing Bayard to Sultan of Zanzibar, 25. vi. 85, E–88, Zanzibar Archives.

[81] For a recent account of these activities, Fritz Ferdinand Müller, *Deutschland-Zanzibar-Ostafrika* (Berlin, 1959), *passim.*

[82] Coupland, *The Exploitation of East Africa*, 437 ff.

[83] Lister to Kirk, 21. v. 86, enclosing Sackville-West to Rosebery, 29. iv. 86; Lister to Kirk, 14. vi. 86, enclosing Bayard to Sackville-West, 6. vi. 86: both in E–91, Zanzibar Archives; Holmwood to Rosebery, 25. vii. 86, E–95, *ibid.;* text in William Malloy, *Treaties . . . Between the United States of America and other Powers* (Washington, 1910), II, 1899–1900.

IV

The newly established economic system in Zanzibar, as it turned out, injured the commerce of the foreign merchants, particularly of those depending on the trade in ivory. The Sultan was now to levy a tax of fifteen per cent of the market price on goods sold on the island, and he shrewdly made it his policy to force up the price of ivory so that he might have a large return. The old and established Indian firms of Zanzibar would not operate under such conditions, and the Sultan appointed a man of his own, Nasser Lilami, to administer the customs.[84] In cooperation with Nasser, Indian merchants who feared to oppose the Sultan bid up the price of ivory in the market to yield the desired profits. Nasser, with the Sultan, believed that the Americans depended so much upon ivory that they would have to accept the new conditions, but they at first refused to compete at all on such terms. When one of the agents, Ropes, discussed the matter with the Sultan, the latter asserted that "he didn't want the new treaties and was satisfied with the old state of things but that now he should *follow them to the letter.*" The outcome was that the price of ivory in Zanzibar rose to two dollars more than its selling price in London.[85]

Ropes and other merchants joined in a protest to the British authorities in Zanzibar in which they complained that Nasser Lilami by "his partiality, injustice and total inability to fill the position which he occupies" was ruining the trade of Zanzibar.[86] The British representative, Holmwood, was in agreement with this: he had already reported that the Sultan had appointed "a promiscuous staff of untrained and irresponsible retainers" to office.[87] But no action beyond this was possible: the Americans simply had to accept the system and Ropes reported, "the whole town stands by to see Pratt [another American trader] and I (through natives) bidding away like mad and running prices up into the skies."[88] By joint action the Americans did get the market somewhat to their interest, but all was still very unsettled when fighting broke out on the mainland in August, 1888, and trading conditions of Zanzibar were completely disorganized.[89]

What trade reports there are, credit American trading interests in the late 1880's with roughly the same volume of business by 1889 as they had

[84] Raffray à M.A.E., 8. ix. 86, Polit., Zanzibar, t. 8. Hollingsworth, *Asians of East Africa*, 21, misses this episode.
[85] Ropes, Jr. to parents, 6. i. 87, 31. ii. 87, 13. iii. 87, Ropes Papers.
[86] Ropes, Jr. to Holmwood, 11. ii. 87, E–98, Zanzibar Archives.
[87] Holmwood to F.O., 23. ix. 86, F.O. 84/1775.
[88] Ropes, Jr. to parents, 31. vii. 87, Ropes Papers.
[89] Ropes, Jr. to parents, 11. iii. 88, 17. vi. 88, *ibid.*

enjoyed ten years earlier,[90] but the traders were not very optimistic about their future. "I am afraid American sheetings are about done here . . . ," and "these little lots by steamer have killed large cargoes by sailing vessel forever," wrote Ropes — and he was an experienced agent.[91] He urged his firm to turn to retail trade in Zanzibar, an idea inspired partly by the fact that Taria Topan was shifting his main interests to commerce with China. Ropes' principals, however, did not adopt this course and kept to the old ways, although other Indian traders had to substitute for Topan.[92] Ropes summed it up in the words, "it looks like the commencement of the afternoon sun for our house," but he kept on trying, nevertheless, and soon found openings in trade in Zanzibar that could help the firm. The Americans, for one thing, increased their activity in the Benadir ports of the Somali coast and secured large profits in the trade there for hides. Then Ropes, looking to the future, came to the conclusion that a German colony in East Africa might not necessarily mean the ruin of his trade, for Zanzibar would remain a center of importance for years, and, if driven to it, he and the other Americans could send agents to the coast under German control to secure the goods needed.[93]

For a time it looked as though Ropes' estimates were correct. The trade to the Benadir and Madagascar gave the mother houses in Zanzibar enough profits to continue operations, in spite of fierce competition from Taria Topan's firm for the hides of the Benadir.[94] In Zanzibar, Topan and the Germans provided the main competition against the Americans. Of the Germans in the ivory trade, Ropes said: "[they] make ivory a science and a life study and must have an advantage over such green horns as our agents usually are." As for Topan, the main competition he offered the Americans was in the market for kerosene.[95] Both challenges were met. By the end of 1887 one-half of the Americans' business was carried on in the hides on the Benadir coast, and in Zanzibar the ivory and kerosene trade remained mainstays of their trade.[96]

[90] Miles to F.O., 19. xii. 87, E 90, Zanzibar Archives; Pratt to S.D., 20. ix. 87, SDA.
[91] Ropes, Jr. to parents, 26. ix. 86, 21. xi. 86, Ropes Papers.
[92] Ropes, Jr. to parents, 13. iii. 87, 8. v. 87, *ibid.*
[93] Ropes, Jr. to parents, 26. vi. 87, *ibid.* Ropes was right as to the future position of Zanzibar; it long remained more important than the Germans desired. See Carl Peters, *Das Deutsch-Ostafrikanische Schutzgebiet* (München und Leipzig, 1895), 282.
[94] Ropes, Jr. to parents, 1, ix. 87, Ropes, Papers.
[95] Ropes, Jr. to parents, 29. ix. 87, *ibid.*
[96] Ropes, Jr. to parents, 23. x. 87, 20. xi. 87, 18. xii. 87, *ibid.* Kerosene aided American traders in other parts of Africa also; for a report referring to this trade in Angola, see "Report on Mossamedes and District," 10. vi. 89, F.O. 63/1217.

Then came the outbreak of hostilities against the Germans on the East African coast. By November, 1888, the trade from the African coast had dropped to one-tenth of its former volume, and all traders suffered accordingly.[97] A good picture of conditions in Zanzibar during the war on the coast is given in the despatches of an English-born reporter of the *New York World*, Thomas Stevens:

> In spite of the competition of the Bombay mills, and of Russian petroleum and cheap German imitations of American goods, so great is the preference for American articles on the east coast of Africa that the American merchants are well content to stand on their own merits and ask no favors . . . Very naturally the American merchants regard with dismay the process of gobbling up that has been going on about them for the past four years, lessening the area of unrestricted trade that, commercially speaking, belongs to them as much as to the people who have taken possession of it. Already the vast machinery of their splendid trade is half paralysed, and the present state of affairs is believed to be the shadow of American extinction here, unless some action in their behalf is promptly taken by the authorities at Washington. . . . A bold stand taken by the United States Government against the gobbling up of this Benadir Coast, or of the islands of Zanzibar and Pemba would be highly acceptable, both to the Sultan of Zanzibar and to the American citizens with such vast interests here. By all means let it be done, both as a matter of common justice to American citizens as well as for the salvation of what prestige and profit remains to us in E. Africa.[98]

This plea for action, and others like it, found no support in Washington. A few American warships were sent on occasion to show the flag, and although the Sultan spared no effort in receiving their commanders, they were never given orders for any action in the area.[99] To Ropes, the American position in Zanzibar had fallen "to a fifth-rate, one-horse, second-class show run by a half breed!"[100] The war on the coast only increased his bitterness: "The U.S. Government," he went on, "is no government for commercial people and especially for those who live abroad."[101]

[97] Ropes, Jr. to parents, 18. xi. 88, Ropes Papers.

[98] Stevens' letter of 26. ii. 89 in the *New York World*, 21. iv. 89.

[99] *Ibid.*; Ropes, Jr. to parents, 13. iii. 87, Ropes Papers. In this letter Ropes gives an interesting description of Stanley, then preparing for his Emin Pasha expedition: "He looks well, dresses well and carries himself with the jaunty swagger of a man who cares for nothing or nobody. He seems to be like a man in a dream, in conversation he never enthuses except over the Congo Country and is the hardest man to talk to I have ever met . . ."

[100] Ropes, Jr. to parents, 1. vii. 88, *ibid.* The "half breed" was a Portuguese-American agent of a rival firm.

[101] Ropes, Jr. to parents, 3. ix. 88, *ibid.*

The State Department's attitude remained consistently clear. Thus, the British Consul related that when a new Sultan came into office following the death of Sayyid Barghash, the American representative telegraphed the news to Washington; but he was told the cost of sending the news was to be deducted from his salary since such action was "unnecessary" for an American diplomat in Zanzibar.[102]

This attitude did not prevent the local American residents from attempting to play a larger role than their orders allowed. Seth A. Pratt, an American Consul described by the British representative as "a vulgar, pushing fellow, anxious to make his position felt in Zanzibar politics," became involved, it was said, in one interesting scheme: he talked the Sultan into ceding all of his island but the city of Zanzibar to the United States in order to save it from the European powers.[103] Needless to say, the plan, if true, was not communicated to the State Department! Pratt did, at least, make a final plea to Washington for aid:

> I trust that the Department may see its way clear to call a halt in the direction of European occupation of this coast; since otherwise the Americans engaged in that trade will suffer a great loss, and perhaps be compelled to retire altogether from this hitherto profitable field of operations.[104]

The State Department of course did nothing in a place so far away from the United States, and of no interest except to a few traders. All of East Africa passed under European rule and the American merchants had to meet the new conditions as best they could. As usual, they reacted vigorously.

In the 1890's ivory and hides remained the chief American exports. In 1895, what might have been the biggest ivory shipment ever put on board, left Zanzibar for New York: 355 tusks, weighing 22,307 pounds and worth £13,300.[105] The trade in American cloth commanded a steady outlet in the interior. In Buganda, for example, only American cloth was acceptable, in spite of British efforts to substitute cloth of their own country.[106] The other American import, kerosene, kept its important po-

[102] Euan Smith Note, ?. vi. 89, F.O., 84/1979.

[103] Portal to Salisbury, 13. vi. 89, *ibid.*

[104] Pratt to S.D., 23. vii. 90, SDA. See also an interview of the reporter, Stevens, with the Sultan on the subject of American aid in the *New York World*, 28. iv. 89.

[105] "Review of the Year in East Africa," *The Gazette for Zanzibar and East Africa*, 4. i. 93; for the ivory shipment, *ibid.*, 30. x. 95.

[106] Perham, *Lugard Diaries*, II, 180; statement of Bishop Hanlon, *The Gaz. for Z. and E.A.*, 4. xii. 95.

sition and made up about one-half of the American yearly total.[107] Nevertheless, only one American firm remained at the end of this decade, for, by now, the mainland ports were replacing Zanzibar as trading centers. The Salem house of Ropes, Emmerton and Co. left Zanzibar and a single New York firm took over the American business.[108]

Conditions remained about the same as the early twentieth century opened. Americans now took about five per cent of the Zanzibar trade, and tapped the trade of British East Africa through agents sent to Mombasa.[109] All this was a very minor activity, of course, and the State Department took less and less interest in it. In fact, in 1894 the Department closed the Consulate in Zanzibar, the quarrels of the American firms becoming too trying for the Washington officials. But the few Americans there needed protection; moreover, the Sultan wished it reopened. It was set up again in 1895, but trade was clearly its only function.[110] When one Consul, R. Dorsey Mohun, reported on a palace revolution, he was told that "British or German motives do not concern you, whose only function is, should emergency arise, protection to American interests." [111]

The Americans then gradually faded out and the United States in 1907 agreed to end its extraterritorial rights in Zanzibar.[112] Finally, in 1915 the Secretary of State, Bryan, telegraphed: "Close office Zanzibar, ship furniture, as chairs etc. to Mombasa, where you will establish consulate." [113]

So ended the long chapter of American interests in Zanzibar. American traders first came in the early nineteenth century; then one of these trading-diplomats concluded a treaty for Zanzibar's first consulate in 1833. Until the Civil War, American traders dominated the markets of Zanzibar. Thereafter their course was beset with difficulties, most of which they overcame. It was the European occupation of East Africa which put an end to Zanzibar's importance and occasioned the shifting of the main commerce to the mainland.

[107] Piat, "Rapport sur le commerce et le navigation du port de Zanzibar en 1897," 20. ii. 98, Corr. Comm. Zanz., t. 8.

[108] Billheimer to S.D., 19. iv. 98, SDA.

[109] H. Brode, *British and German East Africa* (London, 1911), 144; Ralph M. Odell, *Cotton Goods in British East Africa, Uganda, Zanzibar, and German East Africa* (Washington, 1914), *passim;* Kenneth Ingham, *The Making of Modern Uganda* (London, 1958), 114.

[110] Uhl to Allen, 14. ix. 94; Allen to Strobel, 14. iii. 94, 23. ix. 94, 1. xii. 94; Mohun to S.D., 12. viii. 95: all in SDA.

[111] Olney to Mohun, telegram of 12. x. 96, *ibid.* Mohun has an excellent set of photographs of the damage caused by this abortive revolution in SDA.

[112] Sarle to Wilson, 30. iv. 07, *ibid.*

[113] Bryan to Hays, 12. ii. 15, *ibid.*

The Holy Ghost Mission in East Africa: 1858–1890

This study recounts the story of the first permanent mission in present-day Tanganyika, that of the French Roman Catholic Order of the Holy Ghost [1] — whose headquarters at Bagamoyo were "generally admitted to be the finest mission station in the world" [2] — against the background of the great changes wrought in East Africa by Europeans in the last half of the nineteenth century.

I

The Roman Catholic Church had not been represented in East Africa since the days of the Portuguese, but a revival of interest came in the mid-nineteenth century when knowledge of the region began to spread in Europe. The idea of a Catholic mission in East Africa first occurred, apparently, to Léon des Avanchers, a missionary who was to serve long years in Abyssinia. Arriving in Zanzibar in March, 1858, he was delighted with the ease with which he secured letters of safe conduct from the Sultan for travel among the Galla and told the French Consul he would like to establish a hospital in Zanzibar. This would be not only a token of gratitude but a useful stopping-place for missionaries passing through. The Consul, Cochet, was more than willing to endorse the proposal since an establishment of this sort would boost French prestige in the island and do so by means which, being non-political, would not arouse the suspicions of Sultan Majid. When Cochet told Majid of the idea, the latter accepted with alacrity. The Consul then wrote to the Ministry of Foreign Affairs to determine its interest in the matter. But a quarrel between Cochet and Avanchers prevented its realization.

An over-zealous missionary, Avanchers, had made himself unpopular in Zanzibar by his denunciations of Islam, yet the Consul, though upset, had no serious difficulties with him until a quarrel over a slave girl erupted.

[1] This is the name customarily used; the full name of the order, as given in their journal, was La Congrégation du St. Esprit et de l'Imé. Cœur de Marie.
[2] *The Gazette for Zanzibar and East Africa*, 31. viii. 92.

In June, 1858, a French ship from Réunion came to Zanzibar to recruit "free" workers for the French island.[3] Majid protested that this would violate his treaties with Britain and the Consul did not contest his decision. Avanchers, however, so Cochet learned, had bought a slave girl and wished to send her to a French mission and when the Consul insisted the girl must be returned, Avanchers refused, for he had baptized her and so would not consent to her return to Muslim owners. This reasoning did not impress Cochet: he was convinced that the girl had no real knowledge of Christianity and that Avanchers' behavior was "contrary to the morality of our religion as well as to the political interest of the government." Avanchers would not agree; he maintained that baptism made her a French subject. The matter was finally solved, – though it left bad blood between the Consul and the missionary – when Cochet received permission from the Sultan to send the girl to the French mission in Réunion. More quarrels followed and Cochet gave an ultimatum to the missionary that if there were one more difficulty he would withdraw his protection. Avanchers then coolly revealed that he really was not French at all – he was from Piédmont – and did not need his protection![4] Their quarrels were referred to France by both men and the government in the end upheld its representative.[5]

Fortunately for the future of Catholic missions in East Africa, a new priest, Abbé Fava, arrived in Zanzibar in 1858 who got on peaceably with the representative of France. The Abbé had been sent by Bishop Maupoint of Réunion on a trip along the East African coast to determine the best location for a mission station. Fava at first thought of Mozambique, but changed his mind because of the many restrictions the Portuguese placed on foreign visitors. He was much impressed with Zanzibar, and had a very pleasant meeting with Majid. As a result, Cochet wrote to Paris that Fava was on his way there and would probably approach the government about the establishment of a mission in Zanzibar.[6] Fava did so. And so, in 1860, the Comte de Chasseloup-Laubat, Minister for Algeria and the Colonies, informed the Ministry of Foreign Affairs that Bishop Maupoint wished to found a religious establishment on the east coast of Africa whose principal purpose was to be to redeem slaves and

[3] For a statement of this problem, R. Coupland, *East Africa and its Invaders* (Oxford, 1938), 443.

[4] Cochet à M.A.E., 25. vii. 58, with enclosures, Correspondance Commercial, Zanzibar, t. 2, Ministère des Affaires Étrangères, Paris [hereafter M.A.E.].

[5] Memo on Avanchers à M.A.E., 8. viii. 58, Mascate, t. 1, M.A.E.

[6] Cochet à M.A.E., 26. viii. 58, with enclosures, *ibid.*

then to teach them Christianity. Chasseloup-Laubat gave his full support to this venture, as one that would make the name of France known in an area where hitherto there had been little contact with France. He did have one reservation, however: fear that the mission might send the former slaves it bought to French colonies, once they had been sufficiently trained by the priests. This would lead to trouble with the British and must be avoided. But the mission gave assurances, and therefore received the full backing of the government.[7]

Chasseloup-Laubat had good cause to be suspicious of a connection between the mission and the authorities of Réunion over the disposal of freed slaves. For one thing, an agreement came to light for delivery to the Governor of Réunion of the products of the mission.[8] Secondly, Abbé Fava himself noted that the Governor had given a subsidy of 15,000 francs toward the establishment of the mission,[9] and it seemed logical that the authorities at Réunion hoped that the new institution might aid them in solving the ever-present problem of a shortage of labor on their island. The attitude of the French government remained firm, however, and no slaves ever went from the mission to Réunion.

In June, 1860, Fava returned to Zanzibar, and with the aid of the new French representative, Derché, asked the Sultan for permission to found a mission. The latter readily perceived the educational benefits it would bring to Zanzibar and gave his assent at once.[10] Fava went immediately to work; he found a building for the mission, and, then, with the preliminaries accomplished, he left for Réunion to gather the necessary men and materials. He tried to interest the French government in his project by offering the use of his newly-found house as a hospital for French sailors and as a depot of provisions for French vessels.[11] On his return from Réunion, in December, 1860, accompanied by a group of priests and sisters, and a medical man of the French navy, he was soon able, with the generous aid of the Consul and officers of the French navy, to set schools, workshops, and a hospital in operation. Almost at once, the French mission became very popular with the people of Zanzibar.[12]

[7] R. P. Horner, "De Bagamoyo à l'Oukami," *Bulletin de la Société de Géographie,* 6e–16 (1873), 125–26; Chasseloup-Laubat à M.A.E., 3. ii. 60, enclosing Chasseloup-Laubat à Maupoint, 3. ii. 60, Politique, Zanzibar, t. 2, M.A.E.

[8] Piat à Flourens, 18. vii. 87, *ibid.,* t. 9.

[9] Fava à Maupoint, 25. vii. 61, *Revue Maritime et Coloniale,* IV (1862), 232.

[10] Derché à Thouvenel, 30. iv. 60, 15. vi. 60, 25. viii. 60, Politique, Zanz., t. 2.

[11] Min. Alg. et Cols. à M.A.E., 20. x. 60, enclosing Fava à Min. Alg. et Cols., 16. vii. 60, *ibid.*

[12] Fava à Maupoint, 25. vii. 61, *Rev. Marit. et Col.,* IV (1862), 232 ff.

All this occurred in a time of acute local Anglo-French rivalry.[13] The British Consul, Rigby, an imperious man who interpreted the new mission as an effort of the French to take over Zanzibar sent home alarming reports: that the buildings were too large for any reasonable needs, that they looked more like "a barrack or fortress than a regular establishment," and that they could serve as a military base.[14] Lord Cowley, the British ambassador, drew these charges to the attention of the French, stressing the fact that his nation aimed to keep Zanzibar independent, and asking for the objectives of the new enterprise.[15] The French reply pointed out that Rigby's reports were exaggerated – which was true – and that they favored the independence of Zanzibar as much as Britain, and would be interested in any British proposal to make it secure.[16]

Negotiations followed over the nature of a guarantee of Zanzibar's independence. The French had no thought of securing any undue advantage in these negotiations, and rather worked to get the British in a position where they could not seize the island. The British took a similar position. In the words of the American Consul, "Each thinks the other's Government has designs upon this island." [17]

The British decided that the borders of the territory to be guaranteed should not be defined, since this would imply the guarantee covered them, and sought merely "a declaration pledging themselves mutually to respect the independence of the two Sultans, which would naturally infer a pledge from both governments that they would seek no territorial advantages in the dominions of the sovereigns of Zanzibar and Muscat." The French had no such designs and the two powers signed the declaration on March 10, 1862.[18] It stood until German expansion in East Africa caused a change in the policy of the two states.

In Zanzibar, meanwhile, the mission and the French Consul were in conflict. Derché became suspicious of Fava when the latter refused all his suggestions that they visit the Sultan of Zanzibar; the Consul insisted that any such meeting should be arranged by him, and he should accom-

[13] See R. Coupland, *The Exploitation of East Africa, 1856–1890* (London, 1939), 14 ff. The French archives show that France was not as interested in Zanzibar as Coupland makes them appear in this section.

[14] Rigby to Russell, 1. vii. 61, F.O. 54/18, Public Record Office, London.

[15] Note verbale, Lord Cowley, 2. x. 61, Polit. Zanz., t. 2.

[16] Note verbale, to Lord Cowley, 5. x. 61, *ibid.*

[17] Mansfield to Cass, 18. iv. 59, Foreign Affairs Section, National Archives, Washington, D.C.

[18] Memo, –. xi. 61; Chasseloup-Laubat à M.A.E., 29. xi. 61, with enclosures; both in Polit. Zanz., t. 2. Cowley to Thouvenel, 27. i. 62, *ibid.*, t. 3.

pany the priest. His suspicions were well-founded, for he learned that Fava was seeing the Sultan on his own, and, to the Abbé's exasperation, he had the Sultan promise to forbid clandestine meetings. The French government supported Derché in this dispute, making it clear they had no undue plans to secure influence in Zanzibar.[19]

In May, 1862, Fava was ready to get on with the real work of the mission. He informed the French representative, Jablonski, that he intended to look for a location for a second mission station on the mainland. Jablonski went to the Sultan with this plan and received his immediate approval, for Majid was impressed by the mission's work in Zanzibar and saw that any extension would be of much benefit to his dominions. A French party, accompanied by the German explorer, von der Decken, then crossed to Bagamoyo on the coast, opposite Zanzibar. The inhabitants, who had heard of the good work in Zanzibar, were receptive: they sold Fava land and a house. Jablonski reported all this in glowing terms to the Ministry, pointing out that Bagamoyo lay on the trade routes to the interior, and that, consequently, it offered an opportunity for the French to spread their influence and develop their trade on the mainland. He recommended government subsidies to insure that the work there would go on.[20]

II

Before any move was made to the mainland, however, a change occurred in the direction of the Zanzibar mission. The church of Réunion did not have sufficient men and resources to carry on work in East Africa, and thus Bishop Maupoint approached the Holy Ghost Mission to see if they would take over the direction of it. After some delay agreement was reached at the end of 1862; Maupoint remained over-all director for the Zanzibar mission, while the personnel were now to be men of the Holy Ghost Order. Père Horner became their leader and Fava returned to Réunion and entered upon a career of distinction in his church.[21] Horner was to lead the Holy Ghost fathers for seventeen years, and eventually became one of the most respected figures in East Africa.[22]

[19] Derché à Thouvenel, 3. iii. 61, with enclosures; M.A.E. à Derché, 10. vi. 61: *ibid.*, t. 2.
[20] Jablonski à Thouvenel, 20. vi. 62, *ibid.*, t. 3; *Annales de la Propagation de la Foi*, 35 (1863), 135–41.
[21] Joseph Simon, *Pater Anton Horner* (Lauterbourg, 1934), 13–4; *Ann. Prop. Foi*, 36 (1864), 102–03.
[22] For a sketch of his life, *Ann. Prop. Foi*, 52 (1880), 382–88.

Horner arrived in Zanzibar in June, 1863, and at once established good relations with the Sultan; he, in fact, was very impressed with Majid, regretting only that he was not of the Christian faith.[23] In August, he went on to Bagamoyo to inspect Fava's concession, receiving the same warm reception as had the first mission party.[24] Horner, however, did not make an immediate move to the coast, and, instead, concentrated his efforts on improving the mission in Zanzibar. There the schools and workshops continued to expand: in 1866 the mission had one hundred and thirty-six pupils, all bought in the slave markets of Zanzibar. In 1863, the mission also opened the first school for Indians in East Africa. It was supported by contributions from the Indian community and had an Indian teacher, but did not survive for long because the Indians did not supply sufficient funds. Moreover, according to an English missionary, French as the language of instruction was not popular with the Indians.[25] In general, the relations of the mission with the European community remained excellent; the English Consul, according to Horner, even said that he would seek subsidies from his government for the mission but if this was ever actually attempted, it did not succeed.[26]

Horner continued to think of a mission on the mainland and undertook a trip of exploration in 1866, for which the Sultan offered him the use of one of his steamers and paid all the costs. Majid, who was then building in Dar es-Salaam,[27] hoped that Horner would find this the most suitable location. But the French missionary did not find Dar es-Salaam to his liking and returned to Zanzibar without making a final decision. However, on a second trip, this time to Bagamoyo and the villages to the north of it, Horner concluded that Bagamoyo was the best choice because of its closeness to Zanzibar, and asked the Sultan for permission to build there. Although Majid was disappointed that the missionary had not chosen Dar es-Salaam, he offered his full support of the work at Bagamoyo.[28] But all this travelling, as it happened, reduced Horner to an *"état pitoyable,"* and he had to return to France to recover. There he

[23] *Ibid.,* 36 (1864), 124–25. Horner described Majid as "a man of remarkable distinction and of kindness without equal." See *Bulletin General de la Congrégation du St. Esprit et de l'Imé. Cœur de Marie,* VII, 276 [hereafter B.S.E.]

[24] *Ann. Prop. Foi,* 39 (1867), 25–36.

[25] B.S.E., V, 500, 827–32; *Les Missions Catholiques,* I (1868), 65–7; Gertrude Ward, *Letters of Bishop Tozer* (London, 1902), 99; Jablonski à M.A.E., 4. ii. 65, Corres. Comm., Zanz., t. 2.

[26] B.S.E., V, 830.

[27] See Coupland, *The Exploitation of East Africa,* 36–7.

[28] B.S.E., V, 826, 832–51.

pleaded the case for expansion and won the support of his superiors and
the French government — the latter gave the mission a subsidy of 4000
francs.[29]

On his return to Zanzibar Horner found that a move had to be made at
once. Père Baur [30] pointed out that the children of the mission were now
reaching the age for marrying and raising families but this could not be
accomplished without harm to the mission if their charges continued to
live in the Muslim society of Zanzibar. So Horner and Baur crossed over
to Bagamoyo in February, 1868, to begin at last the long hoped-for station. They had, of course, Fava's original concession, but now they discovered that the land was swampy and probably unhealthy. They found
more suitable land, but the Arab owners would sell it only for a highly in-
flated price. Then one of the leading citizens of Bagamoyo came forward
with an offer of a large place near the sea and close to Fava's concession,
and an Indian resident of Bagamoyo sold the mission a nearby house on
reasonable terms.[31]

Horner returned in force in March to inaugurate the new station. But
at these signs of permanent occupation, the Zaramo chiefs of the area began to make difficulties over the land ceded to the mission. The Arabs
took sides with the missionaries and tried to calm the disaffected Africans, but it took a letter from the Sultan and finally his threat of force to
reconcile them.[32]

This was not the least of Horner's problems: local inhabitants, probably
with the indirect support of Arab residents who feared to come out openly
against the wishes of the Sultan, started to plant on mission land. Horner
decided on a *"coup d'état"*; with a party of men he destroyed the crops
and drew a clear boundary about his territory. He gave compensation
for the lost crops so that all who felt they had been injured accepted his
action.[33] One final effort at discouragement of the mission was made by
the Arabs of Bagamoyo: an armed party of Arab slaves invaded the mission territory and forced a group of workers to flee. Horner at once went
to Zanzibar with the request for an unconditional act of cession of the

[29] *B.S.E.*, V, 406, 832.

[30] Baur worked in East Africa over thirty years; he is second only to Horner in importance in the early history of the Holy Ghost Mission.

[31] *B.S.E.*, VI, 296–97, 623–25. Kenneth S. Latourette, *A History of the Expansion
of Christianity* (London, 1955), V, 407, is in error when he says Baur, not Horner,
established the station at Bagamoyo.

[32] *B.S.E.*, VI, 625–28.

[33] *Ibid.*, 1011.

mission property. The Sultan sent a delegation to the town to trace boundaries, but as the delimitation went on the missionaries discovered that they were getting less land than expected. A return trip to Zanzibar by Horner brought no solution; the Sultan, while he agreed that the mission would bring benefits to his dominions, pointed out that if he gave too much to the French, other Europeans would soon seek equal concessions. Things came to such a pass that the French Consul had to intervene. In the end, the mission received six square kilometers of land for permanent occupation — less than the missionaries desired, but a permanent lease was a rare thing on the coast, and the agreement was to their advantage.[34]

While all this bickering was going on, the Fathers in Zanzibar continued undeterred to buy slaves, aided by donations of 300 rupees and 750 rupees from Sultan Majid.[35] A new source of followers for the mission came from the British Consul when he began giving slaves taken from British Indian owners in Zanzibar and promised a large group from the next slaver captured by the Royal Navy. This new source of supply was particularly welcomed, for the price of slaves in Zanzibar rose considerably in the closing years of the 1860's.[36]

Happily, the Holy Ghost Mission continued to stay clear of political intrigue in Zanzibar. The French Consul urged the government to increase its support to offset the growing British influence in Zanzibar but the mission had no direct contact with his scheming, nor was the French government interested in a change of policy, and the Consul's requests for increased financial support were turned down.[37] The missionaries were just as suspicious of the motives of the British in Zanzibar as were the French officials, and made their views quite clear when Britain announced plans for more vigorous measures in East Africa against the slave trade from the Zanzibar dominions to the Arab states of the Arabian Peninsula and Persian Gulf.[38] The mission did not, however, play any role

---

[34] Ibid., VII, 270–72; *Missions Catholiques,* III (1870), 299–300. For a final difficulty about this property, when Barghash became Sultan, see *B.S.E.,* VIII, 767, and *Missions Catholiques,* IV (1871–72), 57–9.

[35] *B.S.E.,* VII, 266, 277. Horner said of such gifts: "Is that not a magnificent action on the part of a Muslim sovereign!"

[36] *Ibid.,* 658–59.

[37] Bure à M.A.E., 29. viii. 68, Corres. Comm., Zanz., t. 2. The government, however, usually gave a subsidy of 4000 francs a year before the Franco-Prussian war—Simon, *Horner,* 16.

[38] Note pour le Ministre, 20. xi. 69, Polit., Zanz., t. 3. This note contained the views of Bishop Maupoint.

in the negotiations leading to the British-Zanzibar treaty of 1873 concerning the slave trade.

And yet Bartle Frere's trip to Zanzibar to represent the British in negotiations concerning the slave trade did have consequences for the French mission. For Frere soon realized that increased effort to stop the slave trade would open up problems of where to land the captured slaves. To his mind the place for that purpose should offer full security and freedom, a climate similar to their home territory, suitability for the growth of "free self-sustaining communities," educational opportunity, and "no inordinate expense to the English Treasury." Zanzibar, he thought, met all these qualifications. While gathering information on which he based his recommendations, Frere visited the Bagamoyo mission and was so impressed with it that he gave the fathers a gift of £200 on behalf of his government. He said of the mission:

> I can suggest no change in the general arrangements of the institution with any view to increase its efficiency as an industrial and civilizing agency, and in that point of view I would warmly recommend it as a model to be followed in any attempt to civilize or evangelize Africa.

Frere concluded that Zanzibar should be the disposal point for freed slaves and that the French as well as the British missions should receive them. Foreseeing opposition on the part of the British to the choice of a foreign mission, he went on to say:

> Objections may very likely be raised to thus encouraging a Roman Catholic institution; but, till our missionary Societies will follow their example, and train up their pupils to be useful citizens, as well as pious Christians, what is to be done? [39]

The authorities in East Africa began to work on Frere's recommendations before any decision on a subsidy for the care of captured slaves was taken in London. Thus in November, 1874, Horner had to write the British Consul that his mission could take no more slaves; they had already received two hundred and fifty since Frere's arrival and were in serious financial difficulties. Prideaux, the British representative, upheld their request and suggested to the Foreign Office, as Frere had earlier, that a

[39] *B.S.E.*, IX, 515–16, 521; Frere to Granville, 25. iii. 73, F.O. 84/1389; Frere to Granville, 3. iv. 73, 5. iv. 73, F.O. 84/1390; Frere to Granville, 7. v. 73, with enclosures, F.O. 84/1391.

bounty of £5 be given for each slave received after February, 1873.[40] John Kirk, then in England, gave full support to the proposal, and stressed the fact that the French mission was more useful than the British since they often took slaves when the British missions would not. He added that a subsidy to the French would be politically useful since it would refute the common accusation that Britain wanted to build centers of influence through the use of freed slaves.[41]

No decision was taken in spite of Kirk's recommendations. He kept pressing the Foreign Office in 1875 and 1876 and won some of the officials to his views. Lord Derby, in a note on a dispatch from Kirk, gave approval, but added: "I do not like what is in effect subsidising these Missions. It is a thing we have never done." One of the Foreign Office officials gave a better interpretation when he countered Derby with the remark: "Is it rather paying them for services performed and reimbursing them for expenses incurred?" [42] In any case, no financial aid was given, and in September, 1876, Kirk reported that in the future he would send all freed slaves to the more distant Natal.[43] However, he continued his requests unabated for years.[44]

Returning to the French missionaries in East Africa, in the year 1875 occurred the only incident to cause armed support to be sent to the station at Bagamoyo. A large group of Zaramo marched on the town, announcing that they planned to pillage it because of a quarrel with the Arab governor. Apparently, the indigenous leaders of Bagamoyo were accustomed to receive a yearly gift of rice, mtama, etc. from the Sultan in recognition of their former ownership of the land. But the gift was delayed in this year because the Sultan was away and the chiefs raised a body of from four to five thousand men to march on the town. The French Consul, on receiving a plea for aid from the missionaries, went to the Zanzibar authorities and the British Consul, who put at his disposal a body of Zanzibari troops and a vessel of the British navy. When these forces arrived the Zaramo withdrew and conflict was avoided. Long ne-

---

[40] Prideaux to Derby, 14. xi. 74, enclosing Horner à Prideaux, 12. xi. 74, F.O. 84/1400.

[41] Note of Kirk, 19. xii. 74, *ibid.* For a sample of the criticism of the system of distribution of freed slaves then in use, see the remarks by Stanley in *The New York Herald*, 23. v. 73 and 2. xii. 74.

[42] Note of Kirk, 2. viii. 75, F.O. 84/1417; Kirk to Derby, 20. vi. 76, with notes by Derby and Pauncefote, F.O. 84/1453.

[43] Kirk to Derby, 21. ix. 76, F.O. 84/1454.

[44] As Kirk to Derby, 14. x. 77, F.O. 84/1486; Kirk to Salisbury, 12. xi. 78, F.O. 84/1515.

gotiations followed with the Zaramo finally coming to terms with the Sultan.[45] The mission was never in serious danger, but the incident is of importance since it shows the fragile hold of the Sultan on the loyalties of the people in a region of vital importance to the trading interests of Zanzibar.

III

In the mid-1870's the Holy Ghost missionaries were ready to branch out into the interior. Earlier, in 1870, Horner and two members of the mission had made a trip into Ukami at the request of Kingaru, one of the local chiefs, a man well disposed to their project. But then came the Franco-Prussian war. It was a serious financial and personal blow to the fathers, especially since many members of the Order of the Holy Ghost were from the lost regions of France. The war and the resulting disorders ended contributions from France to the missionaries for some time. Then a natural disaster added to their woes, the hurricane of 1872, which did great damage to the Bagamoyo area.[46]

By 1876, however, the mission had at last recovered sufficiently to undertake work in Ukami. Horner studied possible locations for expansion, and in August, 1877, he visited Mhonda, near Morogoro, and decided to build there. Missionaries went inland in October, 1877, for the actual building a bit earlier than planned, for British Protestant missionaries had expressed interest in the region. The local population, under the chief, Goso, welcomed the newcomers and the mission station was created with little difficulty.[47] (The new station at Mhonda was a natural extension of the work of the Holy Ghost Mission, but, unlike other missions, the Order had begun with a strong base on the coast, first, and then went inland.) The Christian families at Bagamoyo played an important role in the work since they supplied an African nucleus of workers of much importance in the first days of each new mission.[48]

The established mission at Bagamoyo played a vital part in the new missionary invasion of East Africa that took place in the mid-1870's. The

45 Euan Smith to F.O., 14. viii. 75, E–72, Zanzibar Archives; de Gaspary à Euan Smith, 9. ix. 75, with enclosures, E–70, *ibid.*; de Gaspary à Decazes, 22. ix. 75, with enclosures, Polit., Zanz., t. 4; *Missions Catholiques,* VII (1875), 521–22.

46 *B.S.E.,* VIII, 770–78; Horner, "De Bagamoyo à l'Oukami," 125–39; *Ann. Prop. Foi,* 44 (1872), 418–23.

47 *B.S.E.,* XI, 69 ff, 731–38; *Missions Catholiques,* IX (1877), 604.

48 The fathers once told a French official that they convinced each of their male Christians "that the woman whom they have chosen without consulting him is the only one capable of making him happy, and that marriages of reason always succeed." See Ottavi à M.A.E., 29. v. 91, Polit., Zanz., t. 13.

Roman Catholic White Fathers, of course, profited from their aid,[49] but British Protestant missionaries, too, received advice and medical aid, and, on their side, were usually captivated by the work of the French society; one of them concluded they were "the beau ideal of an African mission home." [50]   A surprising agreement came from this co-operation among the Christians: when in Buganda, a member of the Church Missionary Society told one of the White Fathers that his society and the Holy Ghost Mission had made an agreement in Bagamoyo that neither would interfere in areas where the other was already active. Catholic missions did not usually make such pacts with Protestants, and the White Fathers in Buganda refused to accept it — it was, in any case, not binding on them.[51] But the fact that the Holy Ghost Mission, the first to be in the area, would make this agreement, is one of the demonstrations of the lack of fanaticism in religious matters that characterized the French society in all its East African work.

In 1880, the missionaries of the Holy Ghost felt the need of a station between Bagamoyo and Mhonda, and, accordingly, Père Baur led a party through the tribe of the Doe,[52] an area yet unvisited by Europeans, to the village of Mandera. The chief, Kingaru, gave the usual friendly reception, and in the following January, after Baur had returned to the coast, a party was sent inland for permanent occupation.[53]

The year 1881 brought unlooked-for trouble. An African convert at Mhonda seized a child from a non-Christian family in a dispute over an unpaid debt, which brought on retaliation followed by a period of unsettled conditions and culminating in the death of the friendly chief of Mhonda. Thereupon the Sultan, at the urging of the French Consul, sent a body of troops inland under the direction of the influential Bwana Heri of Sadani,[54] who followed up the threat of force by taking hostages to Zanzibar to ensure peace.[55]

The work of expansion of the Bagamoyo mission from the first enjoyed

[49] For example, Le P. Charmetant, *D'Alger à Zanzibar* (Paris, 1882), 115 ff.

[50] O'Neill to Wright, 12. vii. 76, C. A6/M 1, C.M.S. Archives, London.

[51] Wilson to C.M.S., 21. x. 79, C. A6/O 25, *ibid.*

[52] For this interesting people, Edmund A. Bojarski, "The Last of the Cannibals in Tanganyika," *Tanganyika Notes and Records,* 51 (1958), 227 ff, and the note in *ibid.,* 57 (1961), 238.

[53] B.S.E., XIII, 61–2, 83–4; Le R. P. Baur, *Voyage dans l'Oudé et l'Ouzigoua* (*Zanguebar*) (Lyon, 1882), 31 ff; for a later report of mission activity there, P. Picarda, "Autour de Mandéra," *Missions Catholiques,* XVIII (1886), 184 ff.

[54] For Bwana Heri, Fritz Ferdinand Müller, *Deutschland-Zanzibar-Ostafrika* (Berlin, 1959), 379 ff.

[55] B.S.E., XIII, 74–7; Ledoulx à M.A.E., 26. vii. 81, Corres. Comm., Zanz. t. 4 bis; Ledoulx à M.A.E., 16. iii. 81, 23. iv. 81, Polit., Zanz., t. 5.

the full support of the French officials in Zanzibar. In 1881, the then representative, Ledoulx, tried to get active aid from the French government for further moves to the interior, pointing out that while Paris had stopped subsidies to the mission, the British had provided their missionaries with sufficient funds to found several new stations.[56] But the French government remained unconcerned and refused a regular subsidy, although it made a special grant of 3000 francs in recognition of the good work of the Order.[57] Ledoulx returned to Paris at this time and kept up his importuning for governmental aid to the mission, using the argument that financing the missions was the best way of spreading French influence gradually to the region of the great lakes of Central Africa. Then, if the French ever wanted to make a claim to the land, the missionaries would have laid the basis for it.[58] Again the government refused a regular subsidy, but seemed to accept Ledoulx's reasoning in part in giving another grant of money.[59]

The next inland move of the mission was to the important African center of Morogoro [60] which an expedition visited early in 1881. They found it was ruled by Simba Mwenyi (the name also of her center, whose deceased founder, Kisabengo, was her father), who had been married for a time to one Mwana Gomera. The marriage did not last, due to *"incompatibilité d'humeur,"* as one missionary said, and a problem arose over the respective spheres of the royal pair. The Sultan of Zanzibar decided it, letting Simba Mwenyi keep overall suzerainty while Mwana Gomera was to rule over the district already under his control. Both parties accepted this decision and lived without friction.[61]

Mwana Gomera received the missionaries with friendship and seemed disposed to let them settle there, conditional upon Simba Mwenyi's consent. She was then at Sadani on the coast and so no final arrangements were possible. Meanwhile, the missionaries did visit her younger brother, Kingo, who ruled in her absence, and found him opposed to a mission settlement at first, but when he learned the priests were on good terms with the influential Bwana Heri of Sadani he gave them full permission to set-

[56] Ledoulx à M.A.E., 29. vii. 81, *ibid.*
[57] M.A.E. à Ledoulx, 29. ix. 81, *ibid.*
[58] Ledoulx à M.A.E., 17. viii. 82, *ibid.*, t. 6.
[59] M.A.E. à Ledoulx, 24. viii. 82, *ibid.*
[60] For this center, see Henry M. Stanley, *How I Found Livingstone* (London, 1872), 115–16; *Missions Catholiques*, X (1878), 521, XI (1879), 171.
[61] Baur, *Voyage*, 68 ff; *B.S.E.*, XIII, 97.

tle.[62] Yet when, in October, 1882, a party went inland to build, it turned out that Mwana Gomera had changed his mind. The Arabs around Morogoro might have been responsible, being under the impression that the Sultan was not in favor of a new mission,[63] for when the latter wrote in their favor, all hindrances to their plans ceased.[64] Now, at last, the missionaries had no problems with the African rulers and relations were so cordial that the French Consul gave Simba Mwenyi a gift in the name of France for her services.[65]

Steady progress in the mission field [66] earned for the Holy Ghost Mission an advance within the Roman Catholic Church: the mission was raised to an Apostolic Prefecture at the end of 1883 and R. de Courmont, a missionary and educator, was designated resident bishop.[67] He arrived in East Africa in March, 1884, and he soon won general respect.[68]

IV

The Bishop took office at a trying period for the Holy Ghost missionaries. Their posts were in what had become German territory and while they welcomed European rule they made it clear they would have preferred the British to the Germans; nonetheless, they were ready to cooperate with the new rulers.[69] But the Germans proved difficult to live with. Even before they had any authority on the East African coast, their officials began pressing the mission at Bagamoyo to accept their protection, and, indeed, in April, 1885, Valois, a German naval officer, visited Bagamoyo for that purpose. Père Baur, an Alsatian who had opted for French citizenship after the loss of his homeland to Germany, declined, saying pointedly that the protection of France was sufficient. And when the German Consul-General in Zanzibar, Rohlfs, offered protection to the

[62] Baur, *Voyage*, 68–70, 75.

[63] Baur had noted in 1882 that the Arabs of the coast had been forbidden to sell or cede land to Europeans; this was a secret order, but it was followed. See *B.S.E.*, XIII, 55.

[64] Ledoulx à M.A.E., 4. xi. 82, enclosing Baur à Ledoulx, 28. x. 82, Polit., Zanz., t. 6; *B.S.E.*, XIII, 95–7; Les PP. Baur et LeRoy, *A Travers le Zanguebar* (Tours, 1899), 113 ff.

[65] Ledoulx à M.A.E., 11. x. 84, Polit., Zanz., t. 6.

[66] Two more stations were founded by the end of 1885; Tununguo and Kondoa. See *B.S.E.*, XIII, 1116–17, 1130.

[67] Emonet à M.A.E., 3. xii. 83, Polit., Zanz., t. 6.

[68] The French Consul described him as *"un homme d'une parfaite distinction, d'un esprit libéral et conciliateur."* See Ledoulx à M.A.E., 9. v. 84, *ibid.*

[69] *Ann. Prop. Foi*, 58 (1886), 191; *Missions Catholiques*, XVIII (1886), 414.

Fathers in Zanzibar, he received a similar answer. It might be noted that Valois demonstrated the very lack of respect for the local authorities that was to be a prime cause of the later coastal war against the Germans, for he refused all the honors traditionally given to European visitors and acted in the most discourteous manner possible to the Africans who tried to meet him in friendship.[70]

The question of subsidies for free slaves came up for settlement during this time of increased European rivalry. Kirk reversed his earlier stand and said that only British missionaries should receive compensation for their services and that the French did not deserve aid since the slaves given them really saved them money; otherwise they would have found it necessary to buy them from the Arabs. His recommendations were accepted.[71] A better explanation, perhaps, of his attitude was given by a Protestant missionary at Mombasa: that Kirk had urged him to receive a new shipment of slaves since in "the event of my not taking them he shall be compelled to hand them over to the French mission and that both on religious and political grounds he preferred handing them over to our English mission."[72] This attitude pre-dated the German incursion[73] and the French missionaries appear to have made an effort to win the approval of the British — one British observer, in fact, said they had ceased the practice entirely.[74] Kirk, however, did not accept the change and the custom had to be renewed.[75] Thus, it seems, partisanship was the real reason and not the continued condoning of the buying of slaves for the mission.[76]

The French missionaries managed to stay out of difficulties at first by a careful policy of neutrality. When the British-French-German commission to determine the exact boundaries of the Zanzibar dominions visited East Africa in 1886, they refused to help at all, even as translators.[77] This and the non-participation of France in the division of East Africa, set the

---

[70] Ledoulx à de Freycinet, 21. iv. 85, Polit., Zanz., t. 7.

[71] Kirk to F.O., 8. i. 80, E–93, Zanzibar Archives.

[72] Handford to Lang, 1. xii. 84, G3. A5/O 2, C.M.S. Archives.

[73] See *B.S.E.*, XIV, 615.

[74] William P. Johnson, *My African Reminiscences, 1875–1895* (London, 1898), 39.

[75] *B.S.E.*, XIV, 616.

[76] The French Consul felt that Kirk had no sound grounds for opposing the buying of slaves by missionaries since the numbers affected were so small. See Ledoulx à M.A.E., 23. viii. 81, Polit., Zanz., t. 8. For an opposing view, Roland Oliver, *The Missionary Factor in East Africa* (London, 1952), 22.

[77] Kitchener to Rosebery, 5. vi. 86, enclosing Baur à Kitchener, 23. v. 86, F.O. 84/1799.

missionaries high in the favor of the harassed Sultan.[78] The sentiment was not reciprocated so far as the French government was concerned; Paris refused a new request for financial aid with the statement that there were many other French missions in the world who had not received as much support as that already given to the Holy Ghost Mission in East Africa.[79]

The French missionaries' desire to maintain the national character of their work soon led to serious difficulties with the Germans, who naturally wanted all missions in their territories to teach in their language, even if the missionaries were not German, and who began a harsh campaign to bring them into line. Led by Peters and a Roman Catholic associate of his, von Gravenreuth, the Germans reached agreement with a Catholic order in Bavaria for work in East Africa. They visited Rome in 1887 to ask that the German order might replace the French. No immediate decision was reached,[80] and meantime, von Gravenreuth proceeded to Zanzibar where he made no secret of his preference for a German mission. The French missionaries there were so worried that they undertook negotiations behind the back of the French Consul — it was denied at the time — which led to an agreement between the two parties.[81] But the home authorities of the Holy Ghost Mission did not accept it: they decided to stand on the freedom-of-religion clauses in the Berlin Act of 1885. The negotiations then shifted to Rome for a final decision. During this phase, the Holy Ghost authorities let it be known that they had made no request for French governmental aid. The Ministry welcomed this attitude and was glad to remain in the background, hoping not to rouse the Germans.[82]

Negotiations over this problem had been going on intermittently in Europe since 1885.[83] No progress had been made, but it soon became clear that the German government would not be too harsh on Catholic missionaries, for their cause was championed by the large Catholic party in the *Reichstag*. The result was a law of May, 1886, that modified the old laws against Catholic orders in Germany. From then on, the Holy Ghost Order was permitted to recruit and train missionaries in Germany for work

[78] Piat à Flourens, 11. vii. 87, Polit., Zanz., t. 9.

[79] Raffray à M.A.E., 10. v. 86; M.A.E. à Raffray, 30. viii. 86: *ibid.*, t. 8.

[80] Carl Peters, *Die Gründung von Deutsch-Ostafrika* (Berlin, 1906), 154–55; Piat à Flourens, 18. vii. 87, Polit., Zanz., t. 9.

[81] Piat à Flourens, 18. xi. 87, *ibid.*

[82] Flourens à Lacau, 10. i. 88, *ibid.*; Flourens à de Monbel, 29. x. 87, Rome, St. Siège, t. 1088, M.A.E.

[83] de Monbel à de Freycinet, 18. xi. 85, *ibid.*, t. 1082; Courcel à de Freycinet, 1. xi. 85, 7. xi. 85, Allemagne, t. 67, M.A.E.

in the new German colonies.[84] Negotiations in Rome settled the affair: a decree of 13 November, 1887, divided the German sphere of East Africa so as to provide for the creation of a purely German missionary society. The dividing line on the Coast was the Seventh Parallel: all to the north remained under the jurisdiction of the Holy Ghost Mission. The French order thus lost none of its established localities and had no complaints to make of the settlement.[85]

It must be made clear that this long quarrel did not really harm the Order's relations with the Germans in East Africa. Most Germans continued to praise its work in their sphere,[86] and the partition met with no opposition of consequence in East Africa.[87] There was, however, one handicap, from the point of view of the missionaries: the French Consuls, as always, continued to press for subsidies for the mission, but the fact that it was no longer to spread French influence made it all the easier for the government to refuse.[88] Nevertheless, on the eve of the uprising on the coast against the Germans, affairs, on the whole, looked well for the French missionaries in East Africa. The society remained active in Zanzibar where it had two hospitals for Europeans (who had to pay) and Africans; from 1884 to 1887 they had 7000 visitors. On the mainland things went equally well: the various centers developed in peace, and the individual missionaries were respected by nearly all Africans and Arabs.[89]

This happy situation came to an end in August, 1888, when the population of the coast rose against the inept and brutal German occupation under the terms of the German-Zanzibar agreement of 1888.[90] The German officials when they took over Bagamoyo decided to move the Arab governor's staff flying the flag of Zanzibar to their headquarters, but the population refused to let them interfere with the emblem of the Sultan. The Germans, instead of backing down before this trivial matter became im-

[84] Courcel à de Freycinet, 1. xii. 85, *ibid.*, t. 68; Raindre à de Freycinet, 28. v. 86, *ibid.*, t. 71.

[85] De Monbel à Flourens, 17. xi. 87, 22. xi. 87, Rome, St. Siège, t. 1088; *B.S.E.*, XIV, 370–73.

[86] For example, see statements of Emin Pasha in *Ann. Prop. Foi*, 63 (1891), 462.

[87] The French missionaries made sure of this by aiding the German priests when they arrived in Zanzibar. See *B.S.E.*, XIV, 613.

[88] Ledoulx à M.A.E., 20. vi. 88, Corres. Comm., Zanz., t. 5; M.A.E. à Ledoulx, 31. viii. 88; Ledoulx à MA.E., 3. xi. 88, enclosing de Courmont à Goblet, 1. xi. 88 and de Courmont à Charmes, 1. xi. 88; M.A.E. à Ledoulx, 11. xii. 88: Polit., Zanz., t. 10.

[89] *Ann. Prop. Foi*, 61 (1889), 51–63. See also Lucien Heudebert, *Vers les Grands Lacs de l'Afrique Orientale* (Paris, 1900), 113.

[90] See Norman R. Bennett, "The Arab Power of Tanganyika in the Nineteenth Century" (Boston University, Ph.D., 1961), 182 ff.

portant, sent a party ashore from a warship in the harbor to carry it off by force. As a result, a large body of hostile Africans was drawn to the town.[91] Soon after, hostilities began, first at Pangani and then at Bagamoyo.

The outbreak at Bagamoyo occurred in September. The few Germans on shore now found themselves besieged in their town house. The German vessel in the harbor saved them by landing reinforcements who, with their superior fire-power, cleared the town of rebels.[92] A period of uneasy quiet followed; all trade to the interior was cut off, and the Indian merchants left the town.[93] The quiet ended in December when Bushiri ibn Salim, one of the main leaders of the anti-German forces, established his headquarters outside of Bagamoyo and in vain contested possession of the town with the German forces there. In the ensuing battle, what remained of Bagamoyo from the first outbreak of hostilities was ruined.[94]

During the fighting the mission of the Holy Ghost became a place of refuge for all the non-combatant population of Bagamoyo. In December the missionaries were feeding two thousand people daily; soon it was seven thousand. Even after the end of active hostilities their number did not decrease, for the people feared the Germans and the latter did little to change their attitude. The rebels did no harm to the missionaries or their charges; they even told the French priests that no action would be taken against them in the future since the quarrel was only with Germany.[95] The self-imposed task of caring for the dispossessed was, of course, a heavy burden on the resources of the mission; contributions from private sources in Germany and from Zanzibar allowed them to carry on, however.[96] But the continued missionary activity in Bagamoyo worried some observers, especially as not all the leaders of the coast peoples against the Germans were as friendly to the Frenchmen as Bushiri.[97] And the missionaries feared for the safety of the refugees. They had the French Consul ask the Sultan for the use of a steamer to transfer the refu-

[91] Euan Smith to Salisbury, 21. viii. 88, 22. viii. 88, 25. viii. 88, F.O. 84/1908; Raindre à Goblet, 15. x. 88, Allemagne, t. 84.

[92] Churchill to Euan Smith, 25. ix. 88, E–105, Zanzibar Archives; Euan Smith to Salisbury, 25. ix. 88, F.O. 84/1909.

[93] Euan Smith to Salisbury, 4. x. 88, 20. xi. 88, F.O. 84/1909 and 84/1910 respectively.

[94] Euan Smith to Salisbury, 14. xii. 88, F.O. 84/1911.

[95] *B.S.E.*, XV, 68, 711; Lacau à M.A.E., 29. x. 88, Corres. Comm., Zanz., t. 6.

[96] *B.S.E.*, XV, 228, 496; Paul Reichard, *Deutsch-Ostafrika* (Leipzig, 1892), 143–44.

[97] Euan Smith to F.O., 2. ii. 89, E–120, Zanzibar Archives.

gees, particularly the children, to Zanzibar, but he refused. Offers then came from British and German sources, but the French Consul would not allow the missionaries to accept them, lest it would lead the rebels to associate the Fathers with the two imperial powers.[98] Thus the missionaries had no alternative but to remain at their vulnerable post in Bagamoyo.

Nothing untoward occurred, however, until the arrival in April of Hermann von Wissmann with African troops. He was worried over the society at Bagamoyo, in view of his forthcoming campaign, and formally announced he was not responsible for the Fathers' safety when they refused to leave.[99] His fears were groundless; although he roundly defeated the rebels near Bagamoyo in early May no ill befell the mission.[100]

With this victory came a rapid improvement in conditions at Bagamoyo. Wissmann tried with some success to reopen trade with the interior, and to this end with the aid of the British representative in Zanzibar, he managed to persuade some of the former Indian merchants of the town to return.[101] The last local battle took place at the end of 1889, but it did not imperil the missionaries.[102]

Previous to the defeat of the rebels, the Bagamoyo missionaries had been playing a useful role as intermediaries between the contesting parties, their most valuable service being the securing of the release of four German Roman Catholics captured by Arab rebels. The captives were missionaries, three men and a woman, residing near Dar es-Salaam, in Pugu, which was raided in January, 1889, when the rebels learned it lacked military protection — rather inexplicably, since it housed freed slaves and so was a prime target for attack.

The rebel band at first said it would not ransom the four missionaries for money; rather, the Germans had to evacuate Bagamoyo and Dar es-Salaam as the price of their release. Experienced hands, however, doubted the declaimer of a money ransom, and Père Baur took the lead in efforts to free the missionaries.[103] He learned that Bushiri had taken charge of the missionaries (he had no part in the original raid) and when

[98] Euan Smith to F.O., 11. ii. 80, *ibid.*

[99] Herbette à Spuller, 8. vi. 89, Allemagne, t. 89.

[100] Portal to Salisbury, 16. v. 89, enclosing Michahelles to Portal, 9. v. 89, F.O. 84/1978; Lacau à M.A.E., 29. v. 89, Corres. Comm., Zanz., t. 6.

[101] Portal to Salisbury, 22. vi. 89, 6. vii. 89, F.O. 84/1979.

[102] Barthelemy à M.A.E., 1. xii. 89, Corres. Comm., Zanz., t. 7.

[103] Euan Smith to F.O., 1. ii. 89, E–120, Zanzibar Archives; *Ann. Prop. Foi,* 61 (1889), 304–06.

Baur wrote him concerning their release, he seemed receptive and called the priest to his camp for negotiations.[104] The Arab leader was willing enough to release them for a price, but the negotiations dragged on because of the uncooperative attitude of the chief German officer, Admiral Denhardt, who held the ransom money. The delay reduced the captured missionaries, according to Baur, to a "most pitiable condition." He worked even harder then, and, probably as a result of his reports, finally secured their release. This, in the British representative's opinion, would never have been achieved but for Père Baur's persistence.[105]

A new task then faced the French mission. Some of the British missionaries in the interior were trying to reach the coast, and Bushiri offered to assist them, but, as they soon learned, only at a price, and he held them at his camp until ransom terms were arranged. Baur and his compatriots, again the negotiators, succeeded without much trouble in getting all the British to safety.[106] Unfortunately, the French missionaries received something less than universal thanks: a British missionary insisted on staying at his post at Mpwapwa, to prevent the "devil's version of the Gospel" from reaching his territory, for he saw in the Frenchmen's good offices a Catholic plot to clear the Protestants out of East Africa! [107]

The French priests aided the European powers on the coast in several other ways, notably when the Germans asked the Bagamoyo mission to find out for them Bushiri's terms for a negotiated peace. The Fathers succeeded in learning the facts but mutual distrust apparently stood in the way of a settlement.[108] Yet the behavior of the French missionaries was not always admirable; they abused the trust put in them by the rebel forces by acting as spies for the Germans and doing all they could to pass on useful information to them.[109] This, it must be said, was a natural outcome of the mission's desire for the peaceful administration of East Africa by a Christian power.

The posts of the Holy Ghost Mission in the interior suffered no serious

104 *B.S.E.*, XV, 712.
105 Euan Smith to F.O., 8. ii. 89, E–120; Euan Smith to F.O., 4. iii. 89, 12. iii. 89, E–110: all in Zanzibar Archives.
106 Euan Smith to F.O., 18. iii. 89, *ibid.*; Edwards to Lang, 20. iv. 89, G3. A5/O 6, C.M.S. Archives; Hawes to Salisbury 29, iv. 89, F.O. 84/1978; Portal to Salisbury, 6. v. 89, *ibid.*; Edward F. Russell, *The Life of Charles Alan Smythies* (London, 1898), 142–43; John Roscoe, *Twenty-Five Years in East Africa* (Cambridge, 1921), 37–41.
107 Price to Lang, 4. iv. 89, G3. A5/O 6, C.M.S. Archives.
108 Hawes to Salisbury, 29. iv. 89, F.O. 84/1978.
109 Rochus Schmidt, *Geschichte des Araberaufstandes in Ost-Afrika* (Frankfurt an der Oder, 1892), 31; Müller, *Deutschland-Zanzibar-Ostafrika*, 436, 450.

damage in the war. They did pass through one dangerous period, however, after the defeat of Bushiri by Wissmann in May, 1889. The Arab leader, made bitter by his losses, informed Père Baur that he was very angry over the failure of the missionaries to warn him of German plans, and that in the future he might attack their inland posts and hold the resident missionaries for ransom.[110]   And, in fact, he appeared near Morogoro in July to carry out his threat.   But when he found that the Africans there would give him no support, their chief, Kingo, being particularly firm on the point, he left without harming the station.   Soon after, however, Bushiri attacked and destroyed the German post at Mpwapwa, and caused the C.M.S. missionaries to evacuate their station there.   The Holy Ghost missionaries were worried over this turn of events and fled from some of their weaker stations for a time, but in the end they were left in peace.   The inland visit of Wissmann in September and of other German expeditions later, put an end to the danger from the rebels.[111]

Even during these hostilities, the Holy Ghost Mission continued to expand its work in East Africa.   In November of 1888, Bishop de Courmont, discouraged by the turn of events in the German sphere, asked the British representative in Zanzibar for permission to found stations in British territory.   The Consul, Euan Smith, a great admirer of the work of the French mission, wrote to ask the Imperial British East Africa Company to support the plan.[112]   The French missionaries tried to carry out this expansion, particularly in the vicinity of the Tana River, but floods and other hindrances caused them to abandon their ventures in 1890.[113] Later, however, new efforts were made in the British sphere.[114]   They had plans to branch out, also, into the German sphere, on Mount Kilimanjaro, and received Bushiri's permission to pass there in peace during the early stages of the war.   They did send a party to keep watch during the hostilities, and, when the war was over, established a permanent station.[115]

Once the German victory was achieved in East Africa, the relations of the French mission with the German authorities remained friendly.   Ger-

[110] *B.S.E.*, XV, 284, 677.

[111] *Ibid.*, 424, 677–79, 717–18; *Ann. Prop. Foi*, 62 (1890), 35–43.

[112] Euan Smith to Salisbury, 18. xi. 88, enclosing de Courmont à Euan Smith, 19. xi. 88, F.O. 84/1910.

[113] *B.S.E.*, XV, 745 ff; Barthelemy à M.A.E., I. xii. 89, Corres. Comm., Zanz., t. 7; Euan Smith to Salisbury, 27. i. 90, 13. ii. 90, 17. ii. 90, F.O. 84/2059.

[114] *The Gazette for Zanzibar and East Africa*, 4. i. 93.

[115] *B.S.E.*, XV, 824; Lacau à M.A.E., 1. ii. 89, Corres. Comm., Zanz., t. 7; Herbette à Ribot, 4. iii. 91, Allemagne, t. 101.

man members were gradually integrated into its ranks and all friction came to an end.[116]

Thus concludes a record of thirty years' labor by, perhaps, the most successful mission society in East Africa. By avoiding politics when possible, and by service to all, the Holy Ghost Mission attained the esteem of Europeans, Arabs, and Africans, and thereby escaped many of the difficulties suffered by the other mission societies. The pride of those in East Africa in this, "the finest mission station in the world," as it was called by *The Gazette for Zanzibar and East Africa*, was clearly justified.

[116] See Carl Peters, *Die Deutsch-Ostafrikanische Shutzgebiete* (München und Leipzig, 1895), 250, 260–62, 286–88; Hans Meyer, *Das Deutsch Kolonialreich* (Leipzig und Wien, 1909), 105.

Mwinyi Mtwana and the Sultan of Zanzibar

The precise nature of the influence of the Sultan of Zanzibar in various parts of East Africa during the nineteenth century is difficult to determine. The many Arab and Swahili leaders of the coast and interior regarded him in greatly differing ways — as did Said ibn Salim of Tabora,[1] Bwana Heri of Sadani,[2] and Mwinyi Mtwana of Mduburu. The last-named leader and his contract with the Sultan of Zanzibar to protect Arab caravans passing through the district of Ugogo, are the object of this study.

For the Arabs of Zanzibar, Ugogo had long been dangerous territory which had to be crossed on the route to the interior. Many travellers commented on it as an unfriendly land; Carl Peters, for example, said:

> Of all the countries through which we travelled Ugogo is the ugliest, and, I may add, the most repulsive; and the disposition of the people is in keeping with the character of the country.[3]

More picturesquely, Stanley described the Gogo as "the Irish of Africa — clannish and full of fight."[4] The demands made by these warlike people on Arab travellers became so onerous — in some instances fifteen to twenty per cent of their goods — that the Sultan of Zanzibar apparently decided to take action.[5] The man he chose for the task was Mwinyi Mtwana. Most of those commenting on his background describe him as a man from the coastal regions, a few naming Bagamoyo as his home.[6] Other observers report he was a Muscat Arab, a former slave, or a *mgwana* (Swahili

[1] Norman R. Bennett, "The Arab Power of Tanganyika in the Nineteenth Century" (Boston University, Ph.D., 1961), 11 ff.

[2] Fritz Ferdinand Müller, *Deutschland-Zanzibar-Ostafrika* (Berlin, 1959), 379 ff.

[3] Carl Peters, *New Light on Dark Africa* (London, 1891), 520–21.

[4] Stanley's letter of 4. vii. 71 in *The New York Herald* of 22. xii. 71.

[5] Paul Reichard, *Deutsch-Ostafrika* (Leipzig, 1892), 329.

[6] Norman R. Bennett, "Captain Storms in Tanganyika: 1882–1885," *Tanganyika Notes and Records*, 54 (1960), 53; Kirk to F.O., 10. iii. 81, Q–25, Zanzibar Archives; Jerome Becker, *La Vie en Afrique* (Bruxelles, 1887), I, 140, 160; Reichard, *Ostafrika*, 330; Carl Peters, *Das Deutsch-Ostafrikanische Schutzgebiet* (Munchen und Leipzig, 1895), 242.

— *mwungwana* — a freeman).[7]   An interesting note by an English missionary sets forth that he was the brother of the well-known Swahili leader of Ujiji, Mwinyi Kheri.[8]   The reports that name Mwinyi Mtwana as a Swahili from the coast appear the most reliable: a White Father who knew him well described him as Negro in appearance.[9]

Before entering into agreement with the Sultan, Mwinyi Mtwana had spent much of his life in the interior, mainly in the Ukonongo region of the Nyamwezi territory, where he engaged in trading and fighting on his own account.   Eventually, he fell into debt and, being unable to buy the necessary supplies for his needs, decided to try his luck in a new region of Tanganyika and moved to western Ugogo.[10]   At this point he made the agreement with the Sultan of Zanzibar: the Sultan was to furnish him with a yearly subsidy if he would undertake to protect Arab caravans on their way through Ugogo.   Several Europeans who met Mwinyi Mtwana mention the contract and there seems little reason to doubt its existence.   It would cost the Sultan little and, if successful, increase his profits from trade passing to Zanzibar.   Moreover, a Belgian officer, Becker, who usually was very accurate in his reporting, described Mwinyi Mtwana as a person for whom the Sultan had *"une estime et une affection particulières."*   If this was true, an agreement would have been all the more easy to conclude.[11]

Mwinyi Mtwana then spent several years in the western extremity of Ugogo, building up his forces for a really decisive measure.[12]   There are reports of Arab activity in Ugogo in the early 1870's that might be related to him,[13] but it appears more likely that he began his activity a few years before 1880.   In 1878, as they left Ugogo, a party of White Fathers observed a village of coast people sent by the Sultan of Zanzibar; this could have been Mwinyi Mtwana and his party, although his name is not men-

[7] Adolphe Burdo, *Les Belges dans l'Afrique Centrale de Zanzibar au Tanganika* (Bruxelles, 1886), 258; Lucien Heudebert, *Vers les Grands Lacs de l'Afrique Orientale* (Paris, 1900), 295; Père Schynse, *A Travers l'Afrique avec Stanley et Emin-Pacha* (Paris, 1890), 178.

[8] A. Dodgshun, "From London to Ujiji," entry of 27. xi. 78, L.M.S. Archives, London.   For Mwenyi Kheri, Bennett, "Arab Power of Tanganyika," 40 ff.

[9] P. Menard's letter of 28. vi. 81 in *A l'Assaut des Pays Nègres. Journal des Missionaires d'Alger dans l'Afrique Equatoriale* (Paris, 1884), 325.

[10] Reichard, *Ostafrika*, 330.

[11] Ibid.; Jerome Becker, *La Troisième Expédition Belge* (Bruxelles, n.d.), 80; *A l'Assaut des Pays Negres*, 325; Bennett, "Captain Storms," 53.

[12] Adolphe Burdo, *Les Arabes dans l'Afrique Centrale* (Paris, 1885), 35.

[13] As Verney L. Cameron, *Across Africa* (London, 1877), I, 118–19.

tioned.[14]   A. Dodgshun of the L.M.S. met him in November, 1878, and in 1880 Becker reported that his settlement lay six or seven leagues to the west of the village of Mduburu,[15] the last important stop before the caravans entered the inhospitable Mgunda Mkali region.   The village was under the control of African chiefs who were hostile to Arab travellers,[16] and therefore was a prime target for the Sultan's delegate.   Accordingly, he besieged it from July to August, 1880.

The Swahili leader allied himself with the African chief of nearby Khonko, Mihiama, to increase his forces, but the two together could not take Mduburu unaided.   Fortunately for their plans, a joint expedition of Belgian and German members of the *Association Internationale Africaine* arrived and found their way inland blocked by the war.   When Captain Ramaeckers, Reichard, and others of the European party went to talk matters over with Mwinyi Mtwana, they found him ready to put pressure on them to secure their aid, tactics which put them in a dangerous position and in the end they felt compelled to fall in with his wishes.   Later they justified their actions by declaring that their porters would have deserted if they had been long delayed, and that the chief of Mduburu had to be removed, if there were to be regular trade with the interior of Africa.   With European aid the battle was soon over and Mwinyi Mtwana became the undisputed chief of Mduburu.[17]

This victory appears to have been a major step in the plans of the Sultan to pacify Ugogo,[18] for it provided him with a powerful deputy to protect his interests on an important trade route.   This is precisely the state of things for a few years after the taking of Mduburu.   John Kirk reported on his services,[19] and many travellers remarked with pleasure on Mwinyi Mtwana, this delegate of the Sultan who kept order and was a friend to Europeans and charged them nothing for passing through his district.[20]

[14] P.Levesque, "Dans l'Afrique Orientale," *Bulletin de la Société de Géographie de Lille*, IV (1885), 325.

[15] Dodgshun, "From London to Ujiji," entry of 27. xi. 78; Becker, *La Vie en Afrique*, I, 160.

[16] Burdo's letters of 20. iii. 80 and 26. iii. 80 in *Extraits des Rapports des Voyageurs de l'Association Internationale Africaine* (Bruxelles, 1880), 170, 187; *Les Missions Catholiques*, XI (1879), 335.

[17] *Mittheilungen der Afrikanischen Gesellschaft in Deutschland*, I (1878–79), 179–80; [E. Banning], *L'Association Internationale Africaine et le Comité d'Etudes du Haut-Congo: Travaux et Résultats de Décembre 1877 à Octobre 1882* (Bruxelles, 1882), 10–11; Becker, *La Vie en Afrique*, I, 163 ff; Burdo, *Tanganika*, 413 ff.

[18] This is the impression Mwinyi Mtwana gave in discussions with Europeans; see Bennett, "Captain Storms," 53–4.

[19] Kirk to F.O., 10. iii. 81, Q–25, Zanzibar Archives.

[20] As Becker, *Troisième Expédition*, 80.

Partly because of this, the White Fathers decided to establish an intermediary post on the route to their stations in the interior at Mduburu and for that purpose Père Guillet led a group of priests and lay members of the Order to Mduburu in February, 1881. Mwinyi Mtwana welcomed them and helped them to found their new station, St. Joseph's of Mduburu.[21] But the mission did not prosper. The location proved unhealthy, provisions were scarce, and the war over Mduburu, still in the very recent past, had driven many of the inhabitants away. Thus, not long after, in fact by July, 1882, the missionaries were ordered to evacuate the station for a more favorable location. During their brief stay at Mduburu, the White Fathers seem to have had uniformly good relations with its ruler.[22]

By this time, relations between the Sultan and his deputy were deteriorating. The Swahili leader's ambition grew and he began to act for his own profit. Arab caravans to the interior now had to pay him higher tributes than the Gogo had charged; thus they soon sought new routes inland to escape his heavy duties. Moreover, Mwinyi Mtwana, by the defeat of his former ally, Mihiama, made himself ruler of much of western Ugogo.[23]

Mwinyi Mtwana did not, however, cause difficulties for Europeans. The present writer has not found much information on the latter part of his life, but comments have been left by a few Europeans who did visit him. Roman Catholic missionaries passed through his village in 1885; Mwinyi Mtwana was friendly to them, but they reported him as senile by now. They also noted that a recent Masai raid had resulted in the loss of most of the village cattle.[24] And in February, 1886, a party of French travellers led by the explorer, Révoil, found the flag of Zanzibar flying in Mduburu, but doubted that the chief any longer had any real connection with the Sultan. Tribute was necessary; Mwinyi Mtwana set a figure and no bargaining was allowed but the rate was reasonable and the French-

[21] Ledoulx à M.A.E., 22. xii. 80, 5. iv. 81, 3. vi. 81, 2. vii. 81, Correspondance Commercial, Zanzibar, t. 4 bis, Archives, Ministère des Affaires Étrangères, Paris; *Annales de la Propagation de la Foi*, 55 (1883), 57; *A l'Assaut des Pays Nègres*, 322 ff; T. L. Houdebine et M. Boumier, *Le Capitaine Joubert* (Namur, n.d.), 34–7. For an account of the relations between Leopold of Belgium and Cardinal Lavigerie over the founding of the station, J. Perraudin, "Le Cardinal Lavigerie et Léopold II," *Zaïre*, XI (1957), 901 ff.

[22] Ledoulx à M.A.E., 25. ix. 82, Corres., Comm., Zanz., t. 4 bis. A L.M.S. missionary said of this group: "They certainly show an example of devotion and self sacrifice, for they live on native food which at present is not very plentiful." See Wookey to L.M.S., 24. iv. 81, L.M.S. Archives.

[23] Reichard, *Ostafrika*, 330; Bennett, "Captain Storms," 54.

[24] Mgr. de Courmont, "Seconde Tournée dans le Vicarate Apostolique de Zanguebar," *Missions Catholiques*, XVIII (1886), 615; see also *ibid.*, 583. In 1881 an observer estimated the chief's age at fifty — *A l'Assaut des Pays Nègres*, 325.

men had no complaints. They reported also that the chief, who did not seem senile to them, had in his service a force of 500 men equipped with firearms.[25]

Little information has been uncovered for Mwinyi Mtwana after 1886. In 1890, a White Father mentioned that he had been a source of trouble for ten years, but reported little else.[26] A report of 1891 described Mduburu as surrounded by Africans, fighting to take possession of it, but gives few details.[27] Finally, in 1893, Mwinyi Mtwana, still notorious for his raiding activities, became a serious threat to the Germans by allying with the Hehe, then in rebellion against German rule. An expedition, in March of that year, was sent to end this situation, successfully storming Mduburu. Mwinyi Mtwana was killed in the course of the action.[28]

Here, then, we have the career of Mwinyi Mtwana. He made an agreement with the Sultan to pacify Ugogo; for this task he received subsidies from Zanzibar. However, he at once demonstrated the fundamental weakness of Arab power in East Africa: the Arabs had no feeling of unity, and thought first of building their own personal wealth and influence at the expense of their fellows, as did Mwinyi Mtwana as soon as he achieved some strength at Mduburu. The Sultan in Zanzibar was powerless then to act against him. Perhaps some plan was under consideration in 1882 when Kirk talked to Tippu Tip about pacifying Ugogo, but the latter never took action.[29]

The Sultan did, however, arrange to extend his influence through Ugogo by means of Mwinyi Mtwana, and it would be interesting to learn if other such arrangements were made. The Sultan's relations in East Africa differed depending on which Arab leader was involved, and each must be studied separately before a true picture of the Sultan's influence in Central Africa can be gained.

[25] Heudebert, *Les Grands Lacs,* 268 ff. See Bennett, "Captain Storms," 53–4, for another friendly visit.

[26] Schynse, *À Travers L'Afrique,* 178.

[27] F. Alexis, *Soldats et Missionaries au Congo de 1891 à 1894* (1896), 79.

[28] Lt. Hermann, "Ugogo, das Land und seine Bewohner," *Mittheilungen von Forschungsreisenden und Gelehrten aus den Deutschen Schutzgebieten,* V (1892), 200; Tom v. Prince, *Gegen Araber und Wahehe* (Berlin, 1914), 218–23; *The Gazette for Zanzibar and East Africa,* 10. v. 93.

[29] *Maisha ya Hamed bin Muhammed yaani Tippu Tip* (Supplement to the East Africa Swahili Committee Journals No. 28/2, July 1958 and No. 29/1, January 1959), 141.

APPENDIX I

E. J. Southon, "The History, Country and People of Unyamwezi"
(taken from Southon to L.M.S., 28. iii. 80, L.M.S. Archives)

Unyamwezi . . . is a name given by the people of the East Coast of Africa to a country of ill defined limits, but which may be roughly stated to lie between the parallels 2°.30'.0" to 7°.0'.0" S. Lat. and 31°.30'.0" to 34°.0'.0" E. Long. and having an area of about 55,000 square miles.

Mr. Stanley states that Unyamwezi is a Kinyamwezi word and means "Country of Mwezi," but King Mirambo, who is learned in the ancient lore of the country, says most emphatically, that it has no meaning in Kinyamwezi, for although *mwezi* is the term for moon in that language, as well as in Kiswahili, and *U* is a prefix denoting a country, *nya* is a verb expressing a vulgar action and cannot in any way be associated with the other portions of the word.

I asked King Mirambo from whence the name came. Said he, "The Arabs of Zanzibar and the Banyans and Hindis of Bagamoyo gave the name to all the countries round about here, for they never could understand the difference between Usumbwa, Usui, Usambiro, Usagosi, Ulyankuru and many other kingdoms which in years gone by were separate, and each governed by a different King."

"Why is it called 'The Country of the Moon?'" "O," he replied, "I suppose it is because the Wanyamwezi worship the new moon; they fire off their guns, nowadays, when they first behold it; but formerly there used to be great ceremonies and many rites observed on such an occasion."

I inquired respecting Ukalaganza and its ancient boundaries. I was told that in the present day it is a large country west of Urundi and Uha, but a very long time ago a party of Wakalaganza emigrated from the mother country — which then extended far north of L. Tanganyika — and settled south of the Malagarasi River and gradually spread east and founded Unyanyembe. The fact that Kikalaganza is the language spoken by the natives around and to the south of Unyanyembe, whilst Kisukuma is the universal language from Uyui to the southern shores of Lake Nyanza, would seem to verify this. That the languages are very different is proved by the fact that a native or Urambo, or any of the neighbouring countries, cannot understand the Kikalaganza as spoken in Unyanyembe.

Mirambo says ancient Ugalaganza never extended E. farther than Uha, but he does not know how far N. or W. it might have gone.

Thus Mr. Stanley's belief that ancient Ukalaganza and the present Unyamwezi are one and the same country seems incorrect.

The boundaries I have defined as the limit of Unyamwezi are the result of much inquiry respecting the language spoken, manners, and customs of the people and the general use of the term.

Thus, I find that although speaking Kikalaganza, the natives of Unyan-yembe are universally called Wanyamwezi, and people living far north though called Wasukuma, are in language, manners and customs precisely the same as the natives of Urambo, Usambiro, Usugosi, and other neigh-bouring countries.

Another method of finding boundaries has been to elucidate the limits of Mirambo's conquests, and I find that excepting Unyanyembe and its few possessions, and the Eastern portion of Usukuma, he has subdued and united into one kingdom all the country described as Unyamwezi.

It is hardly to be expected that a very clear history of this interesting country should be found to extend farther back than a few generations; still, it is gratifying to find historical evidence that nearly the whole of Unyamwezi was formerly under one government, and that, that period was not so remote, but individuals can trace their descent from some of the ancient kings.

The account given me by King Mirambo is as follows:

"No one knows," said he "the name of the first king of Usagali — for that was the name of all the country from Nyanza to beyond Unyanyembe and from Usukuma to Uvinza — and even many of those succeeding him, are also forgotten; but Wambamguru, Sabe, and Mongera were some of the kings who lived before the greatest and last of them all, Mshimba, the Lion."

Mshimba appears to have been a veritable Solomon, not only as regards wisdom and magnificence, but he is said to have kept many wives at all of his principal towns, besides great numbers at his capital.

Many traditions and legends respecting this wonderful king were told me, and did space permit, I should be tempted to relate them in full; but I must content myself by saying that they are deeply interesting and wor-thy of an abler pen than mine.

To Mshimba is due the division of the country into petty kingdoms, for of the many children born him in various parts of his dominions, he selected one at each of the principal towns, and gave him authority over the district in which he — the selected ruler — was born.

Probably in his lifetime Mshimba saw his sons fully recognized as legitimate rulers of these sub-kingdoms, for he is reported to have lived to be a very old man, and when he died, no fighting occurred among his sons for possession of the entire kingdom, but each settled down quietly in the district given him.

As many chiefs trace back their descent from Mshimba, and give their pedigrees in precisely the same manner as Mirambo gave his, I should think it extremely probable that this is a true historical account.

Eight generations seem to have passed away since Usagali was a kingdom and Mshimba its last king; but under Mirambo, Unyamwezi bids fair to be a greater power than Usagali ever was, and Mirambo gives great promise of being a wise, energetic and careful monarch, with talents Mshimba himself could not have surpassed.

Mirambo's account of his descent from Mshimba is twofold and is as follows.

'Mshimba, King of Usagali
Kibinga, King of Ulyankuru, son of Mshimba
'Mlolu, King of Ulyankuru, son of Kibinga
'Mkindu, King of Ulyankuru, son of 'Mlolu
Mamoto, King of Ulyankuru, son of 'Mkindu
'Mlindwa, King of Ulyankuru, son of Mamoto
Mangalowa, King of Ulyankuru, son of 'Mlindwa
Kapia, King of Ulyankuru, son of Mangalowa
Kaseri, King of Ulyankuru, son of Kapia
Kasamari, King of Ulyankuru, brother of Kapia
Magunga, King of Ulyankuru, brother of Kapia
Mirambo, King of Ulyankuru, son of Maseri, daughter of Kapia

It is within the memory of many people now living at Ulyankuru how Kapia was killed by a predatory band of Watuta which invaded one of his villages while he was staying there, and all accounts agree in placing that event back about thirty years, and Mirambo himself says he was about the age of his second son, who is now about ten years old. I should judge Mirambo to be quite forty.

Kaseri did not reign long, neither did his two uncles who succeeded

him. The latter must have been old men as Kapia is described as being
very decrepid and having a long white beard. Mirambo has named his
eldest son after his illustrious predecessor, Mshimba, and says he hopes
to leave him a greater inheritance than the ancient Mshimba ever pos-
sessed.

Mirambo's father was king of Uyowe . . . and appears to have been
in no way distinguished by any than ordinary ability. Mirambo was
about eighteen years old when Kasanda his father died.

On his father's side Mirambo's descent is as follows:

> 'Mshimba, King of Usagali
> 'Mbunda, King of Uyowe, son of 'Mshimba
> 'Mkumbi, King of Uyowe, son of 'Mbunda
> 'Mlulwa, King of Uyowe, son of 'Mkumbi
> 'Mgandu, King of Uyowe, son of 'Mlulwa
> 'Mtula, King of Uyowe, son of 'Mgandu
> 'Kasanda, King of Uyowe, son of 'Mtula
> Mirambo, King of Uyowe, son of 'Kasanda

The kings of Uyowe appear to have lived longer lives than those of
Ulyankuru, though. Kapia and Kasanda were contemporaneous, and
between these and Mshimba nearly the same number of kings reigned;
there being six in the former and five in the latter case.

The inheritance of Uyowe which Kasanda left to Mirambo, was of
very humble pretensions, and consisted of six villages, altogether con-
taining a population of about four thousand persons. Ulyankuru, to
which he succeeded about two years after, consisted of five large villages
with a population of about six thousand. The two districts adjoin one
another, and have a radius of not more than ten miles.

Once firmly established as ruler of these united districts, now called
under one name, Urambo, Mirambo began a series of petty wars upon
the neighbouring kingdoms, and so singularly successful was he in
manoeuvring his little army, that he was always victorious, and gradually
extending his operations, he soon had a considerable kingdom, which he
managed on such principles as to firmly unite the various districts into
swearing eternal allegiance to him.

The celerity of his movements, the sagacity of his plans and the ferocity
with which his onslaughts were made, struck terror into the hearts of all
the people for many miles around. No one could tell in what district he

would appear next; today he was at one place, yet yesterday he was forty miles south of it.

His *modus operandi* was as follows. Having planned to attack a certain district, he marched by unfrequented paths quickly to the first of the doomed villages. He generally timed his marches so as to arrive in the night, and about an hour before daybreak a furious assault was made. His warriors scaled the palisades or drove the gates from their fastenings and entering the place quickly made themselves masters of it. The chief of the village was then put to death, if he had not been killed in the conflict, and his immediate successor appointed to rule in his stead. The new chief was required to swear allegiance to Mirambo and a number of youths selected to recruit his army. A few of Mirambo's own men were generally left in each of the newly conquered villages.

Before the alarm could spread, the victorious army was turned in another direction, and another village surprised and taken before the dawn of the next day. In this way whole districts were soon subjugated and the kings summarily disposed of. Mirambo at various intervals returned to his capital, his army being laden with the spoils of the conquered territory.

With a moderation and wisdom seldom seen in a native prince, Mirambo treated his new subjects in such a manner that they soon became his most enthusiastic admirers, and faithful followers. The new chiefs were praised, flattered and extolled to a surprising extent; presents of a valuable kind were given, and promises of future wealth held out to them; until, in their estimation, no one could be more munificent than Mirambo. The commoners were treated in a similar manner; new rights and privileges were given which raised them far above their former degraded serfdom; the only return expected by Mirambo from them was, that each village, according to its capacity, should send him a number of youths to be trained as warriors. On these young men Mirambo bestowed considerable care and attention; he armed them with guns and taught them how to use them; he conspicuously rewarded the brave and loyal; he rigourously punished the cowardly and unfaithful; he even led them himself and was foremost in the conflict; he bore privations of hunger, thirst, and loss of sleep, that they might become hardy and enduring; and in this way, he soon raised the standard of his army to a degree far beyond that of any martial power he was likely to meet.

He himself has told me that he would frequently run fifteen or sixteen miles, capture a village and without stopping for a rest make a rapid march of thirty miles more to another place. As it was always the foremost warriors who get the plunder, his army generally kept well up with himself and he never allowed anyone to outrun him.

These extensive conquests excited the envy of the Arabs of Unyanyembe, who saw in this growing power a serious hindrance to their trade in slaves and ivory. Hence, the first pretext that could be made for engaging him in a war was taken by them and in 1871 finally culminated in open hostilities.

From many sources I have elicited the same story respecting this war, and relating it as Mirambo told it to me, I feel convinced of its truthfulness.

Hamis bin Abdullah, a wealthy Arab living at Tabora, was unfortunate enough to lose a large number of slaves by desertion. These it transpired, fled to Usenge, where they found a refuge with one of Mirambo's newly fledged chiefs.

The knowledge of this having come to the choleric Hamis, he vowed to have his slaves back or annihilate Mirambo and his little army; he, therefore, sent a peremptory message to Mirambo commanding him to deliver up the slaves immediately. On receipt of this, Mirambo sent a reply to the effect that he would do so, and dispatched his most trusty chief, Mana Seria, to Usenge to escort the fugitives back to Tabora.

Mana Seria was a long time gone, and it subsequently transpired that he had been detained by unforeseen circumstances over which he had no control. In the meanwhile, Hamis sent another message, charging Mirambo with conspiring to defraud him of his slaves and threatening immediate war. Mirambo replied that he did not wish for war, and if Hamis would wait a little, his slaves would be returned to him.

Shortly after this, the Arabs attacked Uzimbizo and forced the inhabitants to fly for their lives. Unzali was next attacked and taken, as well as other small villages in the vicinity, but Mirambo and his army were by this time on the road, and overtook the victorious forces under Soud bin Saud, utterly routed them and recovered the spoil, killing many Arabs as related by Mr. Stanley; but here it is necessary to state that the Arab forces were never nearer to Ulyankuru than Unzali, 6 miles S.E.

Mirambo says he was at Ulyankuru when the Arabs attacked Unzali and that he immediately marched against them as above related. Mirambo's famous attack upon Tabora, the tragic death of Hamis bin Abdullah and other Arabs, and his successful retreat to Ulyankuru laden with the spoil taken, are well related by Mr. Stanley, but Mirambo says that had the Arabs left him alone after the death of Hamis bin Abdullah, the instigator of the fight, he should never have continued the war, as he had nothing to gain, but everything to lose.

After his return to Ulyankuru, Mirambo employed his best efforts to render it impregnable to attack. But the Arabs were not satisfied. They attacked Ugundu, a strong place 7 miles E. of Ulyankuru but could not take it. Ukumi and two other villages, however, fell into their hands.

Whilst besieging Ugundu the Arabs had taken few precautions against an attack in the rear, the river Gombe being near at hand, a guard at the ford being deemed sufficient; but Mirambo, taking advantage of this overnight, crossed the river higher up and fell upon them with such vigour that they were utterly routed, and retreated to Unyanyembe in great disorder.

Once more the Arab forces returned the attack, and on this occasion were well organized under Said bin Majid. Ukumbi succumbed to their assault, was sacked and looted, but just at the time when the Arabs thought themselves out of danger, being near Tabora, Mirambo attacked them so fiercely that many were killed and the rest retreated in the best manner they could, leaving their own goods as well as the looted spoil behind them.

After considerable interval the Arabs gave battle once more. They made a vigorous onslaught on Kanoro, captured the place and successfully retreated to Tabora.

Mirambo says he sent a chief with many men against the Arabs, but they could not find an opportunity for a favorable attack, so the Arabs got off unmolested.

Elated with their success, the Arabs issued forth again and were taken in ambush by Mirambo as they were carrying away the spoil from Ukwandi. On this occasion the Arab force was annihilated almost to a man.

Desultory warfare continued for a long time after this last repulse of the Arabs, but the results were generally repeated loss and failure on their side.

At last, after four years from its commencement, the Arabs desired to end the war by making a treaty with Mirambo, and accordingly Marjani, a servant of Said bin Salim's, was sent to negotiate the peace. The terms were soon agreed on and Mana Seria was dispatched to Unyanyembe to ratify the treaty. Peace was then proclaimed to the satisfaction of all parties.

Mirambo says everyone suffered much distress during this war; his people were half starved and were obliged to clothe themselves with skins; and he was heartily glad to cease from fighting. Still, had the Arabs continued the fight, he says he would never have succumbed while a man remained to stand by him. Stones, pieces of copper, iron and even their brass ornaments were used by the Wanyamwezi as ammunition when bullets failed.

A remarkable instance of the energy of Mirambo was exhibited at the beginning of this war. The Arabs had invited the Wavinza to attack Mirambo, but before the Wavinza army could be collected, Mirambo invaded their country — Uvinza — and carried death and desolation through the whole of it, compelling the Sultan 'Mzogera to become tributary to him and even to send a force against the Arabs.

Up till this time Mirambo's conquests had been chiefly in the S., S.E. and West. Now, however, he extended his territory to the shores of Lake Nyanza and the western borders of Usukuma. The Kings of Uha, some of them maintaining an army of 20,000 men, have all fallen before him, though Urundi proved more than a match for him. He says a few more victories will satisfy him and make his kingdom all that he wishes it to be. May Unyamwezi itself soon fall before the victorious banner of the Cross of Christ and all the Wanyamwezi become soldiers of King Jesus!

APPENDIX II

The Price of Ivory in the Zanzibar Market, 1826–1897

The information for this price list is drawn from prices given in the sources used by the author in his three studies on Americans in Zanzibar; the prices noted are for the highest grade of ivory. When possible, the high and low prices of ivory in Zanzibar for each year are given. The prices cited are probably not absolutely accurate since information is not available for all sales, but they do give a general picture of the trend in prices through the years indicated.

Year	Price	Year	Price
1826–27	$27 per frasila (thirty-five pounds)	1867	50–80
		1868	50–80
1828	22	1869	54
1840	29–40	1870	60
1841	27–30	1871	52–02
1842	31	1873	75–135
1843	24–31	1874	65
1844	31–34	1875	80
1845	30–40	1877	84–100
1846	35–36	1878	89
1848	33–37	1879	83–90
1849	35–37	1880	80–111
1850	38–39	1883	140
1851	33–38	1887	116–141
1852	38–43	1888	120–130
1853	45	1889	150
1857	56–58	1891	130
1860	54	1892	172
1864	50	1893	120–180
1865	50	1897	140
1866	44		

The Price of Ivory in the Zanzibar Market, 1823–1897

Index